About the Author

Lee Bird is an Australian memoirist whose debut book, *The Girl at One-Five-Eight*, gives voice to a childhood marked by secrecy, betrayal, and resilience. Growing up in Queensland, Australia, Lee endured emotionally confusing and physically unsafe experiences, carrying truths that often remain hidden. Writing became both a means of survival and a form of reclamation, a way to transform silence into a story.

What makes Lee uniquely qualified to write this memoir is not only living the experience but also the ability to shape it into a narrative that is unflinching, lyrical, and deeply human. By writing with both honesty and compassion, Lee invites readers into a story that feels profoundly personal while also speaking to universal themes of survival, identity, and the search for belonging.

The Girl at
ONE-FIVE-EIGHT

PO Box 105, Narangba Qld 4504, Australia
www.booktreepublishing.com.au

Dedication

Let us find the missing parts of you and me,

I'll be the music of your voice - until you can.

And I'll pull back your curtains, letting your light in

- if you allow me.

Together, let's safely bring us home

Cautionary Note to My Readers

Before you step into these pages, I want you to know something important. Parts of my story touch on domestic violence, childhood trauma, sexual abuse, and the long shadows they cast. Please take care of yourself as you read. Pause when you need to. Breathe. You are more important than any book.

This memoir is written from my own memories and my own heart. As with all lived experiences, especially the painful kind, some moments are sharp, some are blurred, and some have been pieced together over time. To protect the privacy of others, I've changed names, details, places, and identifying features, and in some cases, combined or softened them. This is my story, not anyone else's.

Nothing here is meant to diagnose, advise, or direct. I'm not offering medical, legal, or therapeutic guidance, just sharing what my journey looked like from the inside. If anything in these pages stirs something in you, please reach out to someone qualified who can support you.

Above all, thank you for meeting me here. Thank you for reading with compassion. And if you've walked roads like these yourself, I hope you feel a little less alone.

Author's Note

This book tells the story of a childhood lived inside adult chaos.

It is not a reconstruction of motives, diagnoses, or moral standings.

It is a record of what it was like to grow up inside a family and a wider community shaped by addiction, volatility, silence, performance, and harm.

What follows are scenes from my life between childhood and sixteen. They are told as they were experienced: from the vantage point of a child who did not yet have the language for what she was seeing, but who learned very quickly how to respond to it. These pages do not ask the reader to decide who was right or wrong. They ask only that you notice what a child notices and survives.

The adults in this book were complicated, sometimes loving, sometimes destructive, often both. Many were struggling with addictions of various kinds to alcohol, to control, to appearances, to denial. Some performed well publicly while falling apart privately. Others disappeared emotionally, physically, or both. None of this is offered as an accusation. It is provided as context.

Children do not live inside explanations.

They live inside atmospheres.

I learned early how to read rooms, anticipate moods, manage danger, and make myself smaller or brighter as required. I realised when to be silent, when to be useful, and when to disappear. These were not choices so much as adaptations of the ordinary skills of a child doing her best inside an extraordinary environment.

Some of what is described here will be difficult to read.

It is meant to be.

You may need to put this book down and come back to it later.

You are meant to.

You may recognise people you know, or patterns you have lived with.

You may recognise yourself as a child, as a parent, or as an adult who once believed everything was normal because it had to be.

This book is not a verdict on a family.

It is a portrait of a childhood.

It is also, inevitably, a small study of a community of what can be seen, what is ignored, what is excused, and what is carried quietly by children who grow up learning that endurance is a form of love.

This is not a story about blame.

It is a story about exposure.

This is what the world looked like from the inside.

This is how I learned to survive it.

At the end of some chapters, I include brief unsent letters.

They are not written to be answered.

They are the questions a child carries long after childhood ends.

In telling this story, my story, I hope to bring people together to heal.

Writing this is not about blame, it is about understanding, reclaiming my body and my choices, and naming the experiences that shaped me. My parents were human, limited by their own histories, yet they taught me lessons no one else could.

At a cost.

To my lifelong well-being.

Acknowledgements

I am deeply grateful to those who lifted me, guided me, and reminded me of my worth.

Sometimes knowingly, sometimes without realising how much their presence shaped my survival.

To my children, whose love reminds me daily of life's beauty, joy, and resilience.

Even in our most challenging conversations, when hearts are tested and words are heavy, our bond endures, imperfect, cherished, and entirely ours. I am grateful for every moment we share. And for the love that still carries me. I am forever grateful you were given to me to "raise" as my children.

To my sista Rose-Ann, for your ongoing support and safe harbour in difficult moments; and to Trina and Ken, for love and support, always.

To Sharon and Liam, specifically, for opening your home to me during a challenging time; though not every moment was easy, your kindness made a difference, and for that I am deeply grateful.

To Chris and Amy, for seeing my goodness when I could not, and reminding me I was still here, still worthy.

To my many close friends, Julie, Karen, Vicki, Lyn, Sue, Kerrie, Margaret, Joan and Rick, who believe in my worth - thank you.

To Mr. Harry Watson, whose warmth and kindness gave me a place to breathe, to belong, and to be believed, you made me want to teach, and I did. Your gifts have stayed with me long beyond the classroom.

To my GP, psychiatrists, and the professionals who steadied me when the past threatened to overwhelm and helped me piece myself back together.

To the Berg family for fostering me when a child, further fostering love and belonging inside of me. I love you all.

To Laura Boon, for her inspiration and courage to show me what a professional editing process looks like. Thank goodness for Laura Boon, Editor of *The Girl at 1-5-8*.

I was further inspired to write my memoir due to the works of:

Glennon Doyle, Amanda Doyle, and Abby Wambach, whose voices reminded me I am not too much, and that courage, honesty, and humour are possible even in hard times.

Patrick Tehan, whose work on childhood and intergenerational trauma gave me language for my own experience.

Will Sharpe, whose tender storytelling of mental health inside his films inspired me to tell my own.

Susan and Mario Zaghini, thank you for inspiring and supporting me.

To my Bird family, thank you for showing me how to do family stuff.

Sally Prosser, thank you for coaching me to find my voice.

Katy and Darren More, my mentors, who guided me through the publishing process. I received far more than I signed up for. I am eternally grateful that you see me, all of me.

Each of you has taught me courage, empathy, and the art of continually trying to live fully. You are proof that even in the deepest shadows, light can be found.

Prologue

Unorthodox. Unwanted. Unforgettable.

At the end of an ordinary suburban street stood an unremarkable house: 1-5-8. From the footpath, it looked harmless enough, with veggie patches spilling from their beds, a chicken coop tucked behind the shed, and grass trimmed neat as a school uniform. The curtains stayed drawn, always, guarding whatever lived behind them. Nothing about that house suggested what took place inside. Nothing warned a passerby that the ordinary could be twisted into something else entirely.

To most people, it was just another address on another quiet street.

To me, it was a theatre holding grandiose acts.

Every room was a stage. Every silence concealed a cue. Every doorway led to a scene I didn't realise I had already been cast in. As a child, I walked through that house believing I was only watching. I thought I was climbing the stairs to witness an exciting family show, some drama or wonder I'd been invited to see.

I didn't know I was the main act.

Or the target.

Or both.

Before I could take my place in the audience, I was handed a role with no lines, no warning, and no permission. The script changed daily, sometimes hourly. Improvisation wasn't a skill I learned for fun; it was a requirement for survival. Applause came in the form of making it through the night without incident. Breathing became its own performance.

The kitchen was my classroom.

The dinner table was my stage.

The house taught its lessons in whispers, slammed doors, and the choreography of danger. No university could have offered the education I received at 1-5-8. I learned the art of not dying, the mechanics of silence, and the subtle physics of where to stand and when to disappear. I was trained in human behaviour before I even knew the words for it. Tested in unpredictability and schooled daily in resilience.

And yet, amid the noise and tension, I discovered strange silver linings, small skills sharpened by fear but useful later in unexpected ways. How to breathe through panic. How to turn invisibility into armour. How to carry strength quietly without letting it harden my heart. The hypervigilance that once fractured my body eventually became my guide. It still is. It helps me hear what others don't say. It allows me to read a room the moment I enter. It taught me to find beauty in the details of survival.

Looking back, what came from those years was more than endurance. It was a form of education. Unconventional. Unwanted. Unforgettable. Chaos became its own kind of classroom. Amid the riot and destruction within the family, I learned empathy, adaptability, and grace, lessons drawn from the very moments that tried to break me.

This memoir returns to that house at 1-5-8, not to relive what happened but to walk through it with a voice that no longer trembles. The child who once stood on those makeshift stages didn't stay silent. She found her way out.

She learned to breathe. She began to write. She found her voice.

And this is the story of how she transformed suffering into understanding, vigilance into wisdom, and survival into art.

Shadows and Whispers

Wishing I were in any other kitchen on this Saturday morning, I gripped the broom handle with sweaty hands. I nervously took my place in the very room where conflict was both familiar and expected. My eyes flicked to the white clock on the kitchen bench, watching, counting down. In just under an hour, my parents' longtime friend, Bertie the Bee, would arrive in this kitchen.

Exactly forty-two minutes to go.

Bertie the Bee, along with his mate, Sam the Fizz, were two of the friends my parents treated like family, kind of like "uncles", and I never understand why, since wherever they went, conflict followed.

Leaning on the tall brown broom handle, I swayed, pretending to sweep the kitchen floor. The gentle movement of my body, a secret comfort, steadied me, yet pretending I could breathe properly was anything but a comfort.

Pretending.

It was in our family DNA. Pretending was how we endured, how we each navigated the storm within the walls of 1-5-8. This morning, the theatrics of pretending were on stage in an unscheduled performance. The pitches of the voice, the tone, the precise words chosen to penetrate a soul, to decimate a spirit. My father was frequently the lead, typically the victor.

The kitchen was filled with tension, and the air hung heavier than usual this morning. I could still feel the echoes of my parents' earlier argument: the slamming doors, my sharp breaths, the words twisting in my chest. My father had left in the car, but his absence did not lift the weight. I counted the minutes, waiting for his return at any sudden, unpredictable moment.

The scrape of the broom on the lino floor and the rhythmic click of my mother's knitting needles held me in place, tethered to the fragile calm between the heavy patches of silence. I leaned on the broom as I swept, letting it take some of the weight off me. When I was smaller, the broom had felt almost as tall as I was, a kind of dancing partner I could trust; not today.

Three minutes. The kitchen felt even smaller now, each second pressing against me. I counted quietly, hoping the next minute might bring relief.

Bertie the Bee would arrive carrying six of something, as he always did. Probably beer stubbies or tallies. They would sit at the red kitchen table, drinking together. Again. Bertie the Bee and my mother engaging in their ritual bonding experience.

The sounds of drinking in this kitchen are unlike any other: the zsstt as the bottle is opened, the bottle lid hitting the table, the short hiss as the beer is poured, the long breath out after the long swig. It changed moods very quickly. I learned that this beer, the beer in my house, changed people, creating regular fear that amounted to chaos.

Cigarette smoking would follow, as it did in my house. It seemed that cigarettes, coupled with drinking beer, were a popular combination.

The white, almost transparent cigarette smoke curled through the kitchen like a warning. That pattern of beer, smoke, and unease was part of Bertie the Bee's aura. It filled the room before he spoke, and every nerve in me was ready to fire.

I could already hear the rattling of bottles in the fridge door and the creaking each time he opened it, along with the usual sounds of his predictable theatrical performances. Ashtrays filled quickly, while the smoke continued to thicken in the air. Mother's knitting needles clicked, keeping the house's fragile rhythm. I always counted the minutes, bracing for the shift his presence always brought. And this Saturday morning was no different.

Then, the kitchen felt warmer with increased tension instead of the sun's rays. That tension coiled in every corner, a quiet warning that something would change when he stepped through the door.

Eighteen seconds to go.

Then the knock came, loud, rapid. My heart thudded.

Zero seconds. He's here.

I sat at my mother's side, tracing her hair lightly, careful not to touch the hurt I felt in her presence. She moved slowly this morning.

Bertie stepped inside, tall and well-dressed as always. His expensive leather boots scraped against the lino. I counted every sound: the click of his belt buckle, the rattling of the beer bottles in the brown paper bag, the shuffle of his boots, and the low murmur of his voice as he greeted my mother.

My eyes darted to his face, trained to read every twitch of the mouth, every furrow in his brow, every tightening jaw. I had learned early how to spot tension.

"Hello," he said, voice too loud, full of something I couldn't name. "I brought some photos for you to see. Hi, kiddo." I smiled back.

Fake.

My mother nodded, silent, knitting needles moving. I watched her hands as she made a gesture towards me, a tiny one that let me know she knew I was watching too.

Two minutes in. He unpacked his brown paper bag holding six tallies of beer, putting all but one into the refrigerator door while calling, "Get me an opener, will ya, kiddo?"

Then the wet beer bottle hit the table, and the glasses hit the table, a sound familiar in this kitchen. The lid hit the table, followed by the zsstt of opening the beer bottle, then the pssshh, as the golden liquid formed its usual froth at the top of the tall beer glass.

Bertie the Bee then plonked himself onto the chair at the head of the table, the same chair he always plonked himself onto. My father's chair. Even when my father was home! My chest rose before I knew it. The theatre act was in full rehearsal, and I was rehearsing too; still, invisible, pretending, waiting. As was my mother.

Sixteen minutes in. Then, without warning, he pulled me close, moving me onto his lap. His grip was firm, like he owned me and the air I needed to breathe. The faint scent of his leather jacket pressed against my skin. His cologne was overpowering. I remained still, every nerve alert.

Mother's eyes flicked to me, a subtle nod. Courage enough. I whispered under my breath, "I am here. I am watching."

Minutes stretched; sounds hung heavy in the kitchen: the clatter of photos as he shuffled them like a deck of cards, the steady click of knitting needles, and the occasional conversation. Both adults viewed the photos casually, their eyes shifting quickly between them as they carefully refrained from comment, before packing them back into the envelope.

I shifted slightly, brushing a strand of my mother's hair behind her ear, careful not to draw attention. She did not pull away. He did not let me pull away for long, controlling every move in this morning's performance.

Twenty-one minutes: I heard a car pull up outside, so I jumped up to take a look, springing out of Bertie the Bee's tight grasp. Relief. I sat quietly, invisibly, on the front steps, unsure whether it was safer there or in the kitchen beside my mother.

Thirty-two minutes in: I returned to my mother's side. A brief conversation broke the silence, and the undeniable tension grew. Both Bertie the Bee and my mother looked out the door, through the large open window, not at me.

Seated next to my mother, I slowly smiled at her, then at him, fake but still a smile.

After forty minutes, Bertie the Bee complained that
his chair was bloody uncomfortable. My mother and
I ignored him, pretending not to hear. He said it was
awkward because the owner was a germ: a flea.

He reached out suddenly, pretending to rub something off
the middle of the Laminex table with his thumb. It made
my mother and me flinch.

The clink of his belt buckle as he shifted in his chair, the
familiar glaze in his eyes, and the pace of his drinking
kept me alert. I counted each movement. Each long swig
was followed by a slow breath out.

Forty-two minutes in. The sounds of paper against plastic
were deafening as he checked his pockets for his car keys.
Maybe he was leaving? Everything continued to magnify
in the small kitchen. The faint exhale of my mother and
the subtle sway of his body as he leaned in to pack up his
photos.

Forty-three minutes in. Pressure to perform was high, yet
relief felt close.

Forty-six minutes. His boots scuffed the gravel along the
driveway. A weight lifted from my chest. He had finally
left before my father returned. The terrifying combination
had been avoided, for now.

Mother and I breathed together, our quiet a fragile shield.

But the theatre performances never truly ended. Two acts
this morning already, yet the stage remained open, the
next act always lurking, while I waited for the slightest
cue to perform myself.

-2-

The Theatre of One-Five-Eight

I crouched in the nasturtium patch, leaning against the chain-wire fence, letting my fingers trace the diamonds while my eyes drifted over the wild, bright blooms. The velvety feel of the orange and gold nasturtiums reminded me of my own curls, golden and soft, and of how my mother used to brush and curl each one between her fingers. Seeing that colour felt like a small thread of connection to her, even when the house felt heavy.

The buzzing of bees mingled with the distant barking of dogs and the soft squeak of nearby swings. The owner's high-pitched giggles carried over the fence. Usually, this sound eased me. But on this very morning, I couldn't settle.

Bertie the Bee would be here soon, again! My body was taut, my mind somersaulting, as I already knew the storm he would bring. Every scrape of his shoe on the dirt, every rustle of leaves as he brushed past, every distant hum felt like a warning.

I was trained to analyse every sound. Every click, creak, hum, and whisper carried meaning. They told me exactly what I needed to know about pretending, speaking, and running; when to and when to not.

The sounds of my house kept me either happy and relaxed or frightened on high alert.

The rhythmic clicking of Mother's knitting needles.

The squeak of noisy swings.

The barky dogs two doors up demanding dinner.

Jack Robertson's motor mower humming on the hill.

The Danny Kaye song, spinning on our record player: I loved them all.

All these sounds could shift the room.

And then there were the sounds I dreaded.

The zsstt of a beer lid twisting free.

The pssshh of golden beer filling a glass.

The deafening silence that followed.

Inside the fibro-and-brick house at 1-5-8 Lavandar Avenue, every day felt like a ten-year study of incomplete one-act plays. Father was always the lead actor, self-obsessed. Mother, beautiful and quiet, performed as a supporting actor. And I was the child entertainer, watching, learning to observe, to stay, to vanish, to escape.

These theatre lessons were survival lessons: when to be noisy, when not to be, when to speak, when to look away. Father was in charge. His voice, moods, and violence set the stage. Every scene revolved around him.

I felt the weight of my mother's pain in my chest each time I witnessed the cruelties of his abuse. I wanted to protect her.

I imagined cradling her, tucking her into a warm bed with plump pillows, making her a Milo, and sitting at the end of her bed to see her face, as we did at my cousins' house, to show the kind of love they did. Their home was calmer: soft light, big hugs, adoring goodnight kisses, and laughter spilling from room to room. Clattering spoons, shuffling feet, the low radio hum, the squeak of the swing, and the neighbour yelling, "Hey, come play!" These sounds felt safe.

By the time I was seven, I dreamed of living that life while watching my parents' fits of drama. It was exhausting, confusing, frightening. And educational.

Sometimes Father acted like a tennis player, swinging at Mother's body with a perfect, heavy-handed backhand, the scoreboard in his mind. I learned to watch, anticipate, and read every twitch, pause, and inhale.

Sometimes I escaped to the chain-wire fence, dragging my hand along the diamonds, staring at the nasturtiums blooming wild and bright. A taste of colour, sunshine, and happiness, even if only for a little while. Silence surrounded me, broken only by the buzz of bees, the wind rattling the fence, and distant dogs.

But inside the house, it was very different.

One Saturday morning, I skipped through the neighbourhood, checking why Jack's mower was silent. Joycey giggled at his struggles.

"Jack is bloody useless at fixing mowers!" she whispered. We laughed, my heart lighting up in the sun.

Then, skipping home, I heard it: the thunder of my Father's fury.

I ran into the kitchen. His booming voice filled the room. Bertie the Bee would visit again, and my father was not happy one little bit.

I didn't like it when Bertie visited either. I always felt nervous as he was unpredictable in both his actions and words. I did not want him to be inside this house or near me. He made rude comments, pulled me onto his lap, and would not let go. Mother had told me stories about how he hurt her when she was young. I understood enough to know she did not like him, and Father hated him, too.

Mother insisted, however, that Bertie the Bee would visit and that was all there was to be said. The kitchen tension grew thicker. Father steamed from his nose and mouth. My mother sipped her beer while cigarette smoke curled around her.

Suddenly, the car took off down the driveway. It was Father. I was relieved, hoping he would stay away for a time, especially when Bertie was in the kitchen.

I fled to my nasturtiums, again, my patch of quiet.

Then just as suddenly, the car growled back into the driveway. I jumped up and ran inside to my mother. He was there first.

His arm crossed his chest, then swung forward in a perfect tennis backhand into Mother's face. Her head fell sideways, stiller than ever. I knew I would be next.

"You drunk," he stated, mean and ugly. "You and your drinking mates are all imbeciles, rotten bloody mongrel bastard drunks."

I knew well what was happening due to the ache almost instantly heaving in my chest! I knew it was the fury, his fury. Raging inside the front door.

My head was racing, thinking of my mother. I tried to run, but my body was filled with a swirling kind of jelly, and I felt myself growing weaker. I felt like I was floating above my body, watching the fear from above, like in the song, *Somewhere Over the Rainbow,* where I was no longer inside my skin.

I ran towards her. It felt as though I was standing still, but I kept moving anyway. I could see her, my knowing was right; it was her, she was facing his fire. I saw her back, close to the doorway, her body jolting forwards then backwards. I saw him, heard his thunder.

"Stop! You're hurting me. Why, why, do you do this?" she cried.

"Shut your mouth, you drunk germ!"

The thunder pushed her hard. I heard her hit the timber doorway, crying in pain, begging him to stop.

I reached her with arms stretched out to hold her back, "I've got you, mum!"

She didn't tumble; she held her ground.

His hand grabbed at her arm, and I ducked under to stop him, grappling to balance my mother as he pushed her chest, again and again.

I saw his face, mottled with anger; her face was sad. I pushed between them as he yelled at me to piss off.

"This drunkard, she deserves it, the dirty rotten mongrel bastard drunkard."

Her softer, more vulnerable whimpers were wretched to hear as I stood between them,.

"Stop, Len, you bastard, stop," mother cried out.

He didn't.

Her black eye, already swollen, a cut on her cheek beginning to bleed, she looked beaten, cornered.

He punched her, his hands tight fists, street fighter style. It's like he was hitting someone he didn't know; it's an ego contest. The cut near her eye bled; she couldn't evade any of this aggression, even his quick, antagonistic gestures with his fists. His mind was unable to respond to her verbal pleas. He was killing my mother, he knew it, and she knew it. And I was frightened of it.

Then, his one last ambitious punch struck not my mother but the wooden door trim. Holding his burning wound, yelling in pain, he pushed my mother. She stumbled backwards out of the door, her recoiling body crashing down step after step, finally to lie in silence at the lowermost point of her torment.

I watched her crying in pain and ran to help her. The guilt inside was devastating to me. I didn't save her from him again.

My father had already left the doorway. I hated him, his big chest and his face. I hated the way he looked down at her, then walked away.

I didn't know where he was, and I was not scared of him either right then! It was at that time that I somehow felt

the jolt of my return from over the rainbow, back inside
my skin, and I saw the fear from ground level.

"Mum, are you okay? Mum! Mum? Dad! Dad! I hate
you. I hate you; I hate you!"

"Mum, wake up, wake up!" My mother's eyes opened.

"Are you okay? Mum, are you okay?"

Silence...

I wanted my father to be dead, like gone away forever
dead; I hated him so much.

My mother and I stayed at the bottom of the steps for
a while. I looked away, thinking of blankness and other
things like that. She looked up at the sky. I wondered if
she thinking what I was thinking - nothing and more of
nothingness. Her head must have been so tired and her
body...

I helped her to her feet to walk her slowly to the top of
the six stairs she had just tumbled down.

She said she wanted to sit alone in the kitchen. She
always wanted to be alone.

I noticed the sun was beginning to set.

There were no sounds in the house; it was finally quiet!

I feel okay when the house was silent. My heart was
okay, and my breathing was mostly good when there was
silence.

My mother was safe, and we were safe for a while. My father would not be angry for a while, maybe a few hours or a whole day.

Zsstt.

Petrified, I knelt beside her, resting her head in my hands. Red marks bloomed across her cheek like trophies. He watched, checking his work. She remained still in a different way after he hit her.

I hated the way he stared at her, then walked away.

He swaggered out the front door, chest pumped like a winner, the trophy recipient, leaving the house in the loudness of silence. I followed him, not too closely, screaming out in anger.

"I hate you!" I was ignored this time, thank goodness.

Mother and I stared at the kitchen wall for a long time. This was our thing. Looking at a blank wall for a long time, contemplating life, this life.

"Mum, I am so sad and so sorry when he hits you. I hate him for hurting you. I hate it when he hits me, too."

She looked at my face with curiosity.

"Yeah, but he's only hit you like that once."

Not true.

Was I meant to feel lucky? Was it a competition? My father could put me in his trophy cabinet alongside you, my mother.

Zsstt... pssshh...

The sound of skin hitting skin is one I do not want to hear again. It echoes inside me still.

15

-3-
A Story About a Story

Sitting on the edge of the lounge, I watched and waited. My legs curled under me, hands gripping the soft cushions. Witnessing every act, every scene in the theatre of my father, I wondered if today would bring another vivid performance.

My father's past was a dark theatre of its own. I learned from whispers and stolen glimpses that his childhood had been cruel, full of fear and punishment. The way he moved, and the rage he carried, was not born in our house alone. Watching him, I understood only a part of his anger. The rest was a secret act in the theatre of his life. His theatre was not a show anyone would choose to see. I was sure of that. His inner theatre was the one I watched play out in him every day.

As an adult, I now understand the reasons he is a complex, raging man on fire.

He had no father of his own, but two alcohol-fuelled pseudo-uncles who stumbled through his early life like immoral actors in a shameless play. Their voices and fists, their touches of depravity, were cruel and unpredictable, terrifying. His mother was distant and cold, like the feel of her home. She was wrapped in her own sadness, and left my father to navigate a world that was too much for a young child yet to experience life.

I leaned forward slightly, listening to the quiet of the lounge room, waiting for the sounds I'd grown accustomed to. All was quiet for now.

His childhood home was quiet too, most of the time. It was large, cold, and dark, with long corridors and shadows that seemed to stretch forever. Yet there was a piano, its polished wood gleaming in the dim light with keys of beauty amid the chaos.

Sometimes, when he thought he was alone, he mumbled under his breath. His voice carried a strange theme I did not quite understand. No highlights, entirely lowlights, always with sorrow over menacing characters. It felt to me like a story he could not finish, a deliberately hurtful scene he couldn't change or escape from. I would freeze, breathe deeply, and listen.

From the nasturtium patch outside the front window, I imagined him as that little boy, curling under blankets, trying to be invisible, hearing shouts and feeling bodies too close, things he did not understand. I could almost see the walls of his childhood trapping him, the doors he dared not open, the sounds he learned to fear. Sometimes, I even saw myself in him in those moments when I pressed my hand against the chain wire fence and wished I could disappear.

In addition to his childhood training, a terrifying ripple effect of his boyhood annihilation was knowing that the torture he carried was passed along to us, his own wife and child. I sat on the lino floor, pressing my knees to my chest, listening to every creak in the house. I watched the way his hands moved, the way his voice rose and fell, the quick clench of his jaw. I understood, a little, where it came from. I did not excuse it, but I knew there was a story beneath the story; the fury he couldn't tell, never shared, and maybe didn't even fully understand himself.

Still a child, I watched my mother in the kitchen as she shared small fragments of his story with me during a morning of baking. While we stirred chocolate into a cake batter, she spoke softly, almost as if the words themselves could break.

"He was beaten as a boy, flogged," she said.

I imagined that boy, small and trembling, learning early that silence was safer than speaking. Hiding in corners, that boy grew up to be the lead actor in our home theatre, carrying his own terror and wretchedness, his fists and voice performing what he had learned to survive.

I perched on the edge of the stairs, toes curled on the wooden step, wondering if he remembered being that small boy at all. Did he ever see himself in me, struggling to protect my mother? Did he ever pause and think that maybe the anger wasn't the only way to live? I doubted it. He rarely paused.

And yet, knowing this about him made me curious. I wanted to understand him. I wanted to understand why he became the person he was. What it felt like to carry that much fear and anger inside your body. I wanted answers that were not there, pieces of a puzzle I would never fully complete.

But watching this scene in my mind, both its physical aggression and the emotional tone disgusted me. This type of scene, one I could never bring myself to watch to the end, belonged to my father. The child he had been, the increased adrenaline he had carried, the shush of silence he had learned to obey that was now the act that played behind the curtain of 1-5-8.

I whispered the same word to myself that I'd heard him whisper to himself when I was alone: "Shush."

It was not a command, but a recognition. That boy, that hidden actor, was shaped by everything that followed. I watched. I learned. And I waited for the moment when silence could finally be replaced by something gentler.

I was always in the front row of my father's theatre. Walking into the theatre as an innocent young girl was harrowing. Every glance, every movement, every tone carried meaning. Some days, the performance was familiar and predictable; other days, the acts shifted, surprising and terrifying me. I never knew what would come next. This day might be the same or different. I watched, I waited, I learned. I was always in the audience, always observing, constantly measuring the space between danger and safety.

In my imagination, the theatre walls were covered with heavy red velvet curtains that billowed to the ground. Most times they were open, giving me glimpses of the stage, but sometimes they were drawn, and I could never quite see inside them. He was an actor in every sense of the word, booming or tender, dramatic or cold; his gestures were exaggerated, as if for an invisible audience. Every glance, every smirk, every raised eyebrow was intentional. The purple suit, the crisp white shirt, the red suit, the white ties; everything he wore, including his facial expressions, was part of his façade, his costume, his theatrics. He was a theatre in himself, unpredictable, living the performance as if it were in his blood. In my front-row seat, I learned how to read every act, every rehearsal, every subtle cue that might foretell the next moment.

And so, this life, my life, became another small note bookmarked in a history of brutality and confusion. The fear of my father's demons, the projection onto my mother, and then onto me, was blinding. My mother's sudden, stinging personal remarks took breath from my body, fragments from my innocent soul.

Unlike my parents, I found opportunities to turn my life into one of acceptance and healing. These opportunities for self-growth enable me to live a more fulfilling life in adulthood.

However, I couldn't find my way to safety, not back then, and not until I knew what it, safety, looked like. I do now.

Healing is clear in theory and manageable in practice until the ache erupts inside me, fierce and insistent, and everything becomes more complicated than I have imagined. For me, healing is sitting with my feelings of fear and shame, breathing with and through them as they rise in my body.

This is the rightest, realest, most spot-on-est contemplation of freedom I know of. Freedom for me means owning my origins, messy, chaotic, painful, and unfixable. Words stumble, still. I falter, fail, and sometimes catch them just in time to shape what I mean to say. My world as a child detonated in ways no words could hold, and still I tried. Still, I breathed through it, still I named it, still I claimed it. It was mine to own, all of it.

Freedom, for me, is saying: I have been here. I have survived. I am still mine.

The people I lived with were messy, and I survived the colossal chaos as a messy person. It was a rich and glorious education in fire and shadow, light and storm, wholly mine. These people raised me; they were my family, and I was made from the same stuff as that lot. And I was not. Yet I was born from them. I am neither above nor below them.

Amid the chaotic, calamitous mess of my early years, I received my most valuable education. Ever. I learned the "how-to-do-life-to-survive" stuff from this family in this life, stuff I have not learned anywhere else. The events at 1-5-8 and my role in the mess gave me an extreme education, teaching me skills I could never have imagined, skills I had never seen or applied before.

There would never be an equal school of education to the training at 1-5-8. No university or college would ever be able to finance the insurance to build a theatre like the one at 158 Lavandar Avenue. As there will never be fires allowed inside people, my father's inner inferno cannot be replicated. Living the authentic theatre of a riotously reckless existence to survive uprightly was our face-to-face practical experience, in all its flames, sweat, and screaming madness.

Schooled in every high-level skill to manipulate behaviours to survive my parents' madness, I outsmarted and outran my father to escape him by any means, in critical moments, in a split second.

My pseudo-PhD in life skills was ironic, as it was a degree I never intended to earn.

I'm still studying.

I wore my achievement with quiet pride. I loved it, but I didn't, because I couldn't live it out loud. Along with survival skills, I was trained to hide, to pretend, and to carry the weight of achievement and love for myself and for them, even when it was pretend. Along with survival skills, it was all carried silently because showing them off felt unsafe.

It's a beautiful, bittersweet truth that much of what I learned about life, love, and resilience was discovered in silence, behind closed doors, in the spaces no one could see. That very silence became both a shield and a skill. I understood. I accepted.

I bloody hated it at times.

And yet, through it all, I feel blessed for the lessons. By sharing my story, I aim to bring people together, helping them connect with others, discover their own community, and share with those seeking a deeper understanding.

My story is not special; it was life in my world. And in telling it, I hope we can merge our worlds.

Never will I say thank you to my parents for all my childhood; instead, I say thank you for showing me that there are different kinds of parents and people, and for showing me what life can offer. Thank you for being the unwitting teachers of difficult lessons and bad ideas, the educators of the messy, the complex, and the complicated. You handed me the best volume of an encyclopedia ever, full of experiences I now draw on to navigate my own life and, hopefully, to help others do the same.

Unsent Letter

Dear Father and Mother,

I am so sorry for what you endured in your upbringing.

It must have been very tough for you both.

I can relate; do you know that?

I even hate myself sometimes,

a sad but common thread in childhood trauma

of misplaced blame and loathing.

– 4 –

The Piano

As an eight-year-old, the first photo I ever saw of myself was a baby photo. I remember my mother sitting at the kitchen table with our neighbour, sliding the photograph from a large white paper bag. She held it by its cardboard backing so the neighbour and I could see. It felt stiff in my hands. I loved having it and examining it closely to discover exactly what I looked like as a baby.

It was a large photo, in soft pastel colours, dog-eared at the corners. The way I was dressed made me feel like a member of the royal family. The more I looked, the more spectacular it was.

My mother said the photo was taken when I was eight months old. Seated at the centre of a large table, I wore a bright white romper suit buttoned at the front. I stared at my golden hair, swirled on top of my head, and wondered how long it took my mother to make it stay like that. I loved every smidgen of that image, even though I looked like a boy baby.

Later that day, as I wandered among the nasturtiums in our front yard, I thought about how long it had been since I was eight months old. Why wasn't this photo hanging on our wall in a solid wooden frame, like the ones at my grandmother's house? She had heaps of pictures on her walls! I didn't know the people in them, but I loved their dresses and enjoyed seeing them every time I visited.

Most of her photos were black and white; they weren't coloured, like mine. That was the only reason my photo made me feel like royalty. I couldn't stop looking at it. Not the boy-baby part, everything else.

One peculiar thing I especially noticed about Grandma's photos was the people in them. The ladies looked more like the men standing next to them. Each person had the same short hairstyle, grim faces, straight, shapeless bodies, and pale skin.

"It's the make-up," said Grandma.

I related to the grim faces on her walls; I already knew what unhappiness felt like. I owned both. When I grew up, unlike the people in those photos, I wanted to be a smiling girl, with happiness inside that showed outside.

The lack of smiles in those images felt like the cold, dark silence of Grandma's house. The whole place was a mix of dungeons and light.

I had a favourite spot, though. My best-loved room in her big house was the dining room. It felt grand, like a palace. Red and green carpet covered the floors. Long timber sideboards held framed photos and vases of big red roses. In the middle of the room stood the dark, shiny dining table surrounded by matching chairs. Above it hung a gigantic light, not a chandelier, but almost. It demanded attention.

But the best part was the gleaming black piano.

"It's a grand," said Grandma, as if it held a secret. My family admired it, touching it as if it were priceless.

Against the dining room wall, it held centre stage. Its gleam and presence earned attention on its own.

How cool, I thought, to be important just for existing.

"Pianos are special instruments. This one can do things no other instrument can," said Grandma proudly.

I loved it. It was the most magnificent musical instrument I had ever laid hands on. It stood centre stage in the dining room. My dance teacher had said the same about our concert. We were magnificent, holding everyone's attention, too.

I felt proud of it, that glorious piano, because it was in Grandma's house and was unique.

Sliding my fingers along its tall sides, I daydreamed that one day I could be like the piano, special to my parents, significant, holding centre stage.

But I would not be.

I was not like the piano. I was unheard, unseen, invisible. Not significant. Only my father held centre stage.

At dinner that night, long after I daydreamed, the announcement rang out through the house. That night's meal was one of my most unfavourite meals ever: tripe.

I let out a sharp, high-pitched scream!

I slipped away quietly. Very soon after that, my father's roar rang out through the house: "Get back in here, you rotten bloody mongrel kid!"

I could hear his footsteps approaching my hiding place. He reached behind the lounge chair, pulled my pyjama shirt, and marched me back to the kitchen.

Then I was physically handled and directed to stand stiffly against the cold kitchen wall, in the same spot where he had given his lecture the night before. With eyes fixed on mine and a finger pointing, he listed at least seventeen reasons I was to eat the meal.

As I stared back, I felt my face turning into a semi-circle, a smile.

I was the only thing that mattered. I had my father's attention.

I was like the piano.

Centre stage.

Smiling.

I was just like the piano.

Unsent Letter

Dearest little me

I realise I am a dot connector!

-5-

Midday

Primary school was a tricky place to live out two lives, my inside 1-5-8 life of shame and embarrassment as a kid, protecting my mother and myself from beatings, and in public life, pretending to be a normal girl. I played at being a happy, functioning kid, like everyone else, from a regular suburban family.

Being just eight years old and having to be two girls every day made my head feel… "thick," as if it couldn't fit anything else inside. I did try, though, to be the happy, friendly, functioning, thinking, "on-the-ball" kid all day at school. It felt exhausting, but I tried hard to stay focused on being that kid.

Before I went to school, though, by the time I was four going on five, I already knew something was not right in my house or with me. I was living with loud, noisy, screaming, punchy people in a scary house where I was frightened most of the time.

The grown-ups did not protect me from being hit often, and they acted as if they did not want me. I never felt like a typical kid. I felt like I was half a kid; half of me could breathe, eat, and sleep, but the other half couldn't always think. That half felt empty. I tried to hide that part so I wouldn't look stupid and dumb. I was a kid in

28

a family where, most of the time, I did not matter much to my parents. Sometimes I felt like I was less than half a proper kid, because my father cared about me less than half the time, and that made me feel embarrassed just for being me, for being around, for taking up space, eating their food, needing clothing, all those things. I felt alone, scared, lonely, and ashamed of being me. I was frightened of everything.

I wanted my father to stop hurting me and wanted both my parents to talk nicely to me, be kind to me.

As I was growing up, I longed to be the kind of kid who could make a best friend. I really wanted a best friend, like my friends Debbie and Ann, who were best friends. However, I couldn't see how I could have a best friend because best friends typically came to my house after school to play, and I wasn't bringing any school friends home with me.

Pretending to be a right and proper kid, living my pretend life outside my house and family, became easier as time went on. I grew used to being more friendly and smiley once I was out of my house each school day. I can't pinpoint precisely when the change occurred, but it became easier to cope. Being with my friends at school became a place where I felt the change happening. I belonged in my group of friends; I fitted in, I felt like them, acted like them, and often laughed at the same things they did.

Knowing I had friends to sit with at lunchtime brought me great happiness; having a seat in the classroom all to myself made it feel special. There was a place for me at morning tea time, at lunch time, and at midday, and I was expected to be there. Having a place to be, a place meant for me, where I could be just who I was, helped me be just who I was.

In contrast, I remember being a little kid, there was a
particular time each day when I was not expected to be
anywhere or to be seen. I was required to be invisible: in
fact, at the same time, day after day, at midday.

Midday
The sun no longer shines on the windowsill
Yet the kitchen's still wrapped in its warmth
A mother and her white baby kitten, pure joy
Joy! Or so she thought!

So heart-warming are the ordinary sounds
of a mother preparing the evening meal as she hums
Then the clearing up and the washing up…
It's near, here, the fear,
It's begun: another midday.

Sleeping peacefully
on the large comfortable bed
is the midday ritual
for the weary and distant woman
and the white baby kitten.
Yet not for the child.
She was not an invitee!

Invisible is she, not seen, not someone, not at midday,
She has somewhere to be
Absent from her mother's mind,
not part of her mother's Midday show.
Her torment when the hands of the clock strike twelve,
Her mother will never know.

Head leaning on the doorway,
Then a long, slow slide down the wall as
Her eyes lock on that bed; she cannot look away
Watching her mother, the kitten, the bed,
…then the floor.

In the piercing silence of her midday
Wondering why nothing inside feels okay
to be alone and five
trying to feel calm inside
She is learning to find her brave.

Is there room on the big bed up there?
From the floor, her eyes can see
She wants to be close to her mother
Beside each other
She is sure there is room for three.

Is there something the matter?
Something is so wrong with her
that she could be invisible
like in her story time book?
Yet she can see herself
If her mother would only look!

Back to before right now
in her mother's eyes,
She thinks she saw a longing
Vague and detached,
not beholding nor engaging
her nor anybody.

Now standing on tippytoes
to peer out of the window
Seeing the wind spinning, the petals falling
across the yard, the orange flowers blow,
It is her friends, the nasturtiums, calling.

Grown from the sun,
Honey sweet and delicious in the stem, yet
...Sweeter is the sound of the kitten's cry
waking mother.
She can breathe,
she is safe again,
It's not midday now.

In those times I had nowhere to be, no place that felt like it was truly mine. Invisible, overlooked, left on the floor, watching others share what I longed for.

I learned what it meant to exist without being seen.

Unsent Letter

Dear Mother,

I waited for you to ask me up,

Onto your bed.

You never did.

Was that because you didn't see me?

Or because you did?

– 6 –

Masks

There came a rare and precious time, a place that was mine, a space where I mattered. It began when I met my favourite teacher, Mr. Harry Watson. For three short years, he taught me, and in that brief time, his warmth and sincerity gave me a place to stand, breathe, and belong.

Mr. Watson had something about him I could feel. He took up space in the classroom, filling the air with joy and a sense of peace. He created a sense of safety, which was essential for me. Safe was neither a feeling nor a word I understood much until I met Mr. Watson. He was the opposite of my father, lacking complexity altogether. I started to feel okay, good, not scared, happy, and then safe when I was around him. I came to understand the meaning and feelings associated with "safe."

Safe meant I felt relaxed, another new word I learned. I sometimes forgot I was "the other girl," the one who had to pretend her life was perfect. Safe helped me forget. Safe allowed me to be less vigilant, less hyper-aware of my surroundings. I could lighten up and settle my fragile insides a little. These were new feelings that were soft, like clouds inside, not heavy stuff that weighed me down.

When I made a mistake in my schoolwork, I felt like I had the energy and a happy heart to be okay. I no longer felt stupid, useless, or embarrassed, and I was less worried about how I would cope with the teacher knowing about my blunders. I was no longer overly frightened of being in trouble for the error or worried about a beating, which was my usual pattern of thought when I made a mistake at 1-5-8. Of course, I was not going to be beaten at school, yet my mind automatically took me to that scary place. I did not go there as often.

Mr. Watson's kindness and cheery manner made me realise that my error was simply that, and that it was okay to make errors. This new feeling made me realise I could be myself without feeling the need to pretend to be okay when I wasn't. I remember feeling less hyper-vigilant all day, not so worried about my surroundings, my own thoughts, or my reactions to people at school. This became my new normal at school. It felt like I had a new set of light shoulders, carrying far less weight. My thoughts changed often, yet now I was thinking positive things at school, and it felt so good, different.

As a student in Mr. Watson's classes, I began to feel that I had found the magic thing I had been wishing and hoping for so long. I had met a teacher, a person who saw me for who I was, a kid trying my best to do the right things with what I had.

Mr. Watson was the magic; he showed me he believed I was a good kid, and he had my back. I knew he did. I could feel it. It was hard to describe how I knew, because he spoke quietly and kindly. He was quietly awesome. All the kids in his class adored him.

It became a strange thing, but I could sense something about people, an energy, a feeling for them. I did not know how to explain it. Initially, I felt it, recognised its meaning, and knew it was real. I didn't tell anyone; they would think I was even stupider than my father claimed. But I felt warmth and softness from the friendly people I met, and I also sensed negative feelings and discomfort from others.

These miraculous, magical new feelings helped me understand myself better, which, in turn, strengthened my confidence. As I gained a deeper understanding of people and myself, I began to appreciate my family.

It worked sometimes: my insides didn't shake as often, and my mind could think clearly, making it easier to find answers. I was so excited.

Harry Watson always made the whole class feel that whatever we had to say was important, as he sat on the desk, listening like a big brother. It made my days joyful, and I enjoyed coming to school.

I didn't always have all my schoolbooks, and I think he knew this, yet he never questioned or embarrassed me, nor did he make a scene about my homework. I didn't know which house I'd be in from one night to the next, so homework wasn't on my mind for most of my time after school.

Mr. Watson was different from other teachers. He created a kid community in the classroom, a safe place where we all belonged. He neither handed out misdemeanours nor highlighted any student's lack of ability.

I cherished the time I spent with him as my teacher and still look back at Mr. Watson, knowing he was the miracle I longed for as a child. Mr. Harry Watson inspired me long after I left his care at primary school, well into my career in education. He was and remains my role model. I gave to my students in the same way Harry gave to me: a joy of learning and a joyful way to learn.

For many years, I wanted to find Mr. Watson in my adult life to express my sincere gratitude; to somehow let him know he was the miracle I had longed for, the person who gave me hope.

Unsent Letter

Dear Mr. Watson,

I actually didn't believe in magic,

until now.

-7-
Inside Belonging

That beautiful feeling of belonging became part of my everyday world, a place where my real life lived. I felt alive, seen, and like I mattered, and I wanted more of that safety and joy. Belonging was new and wonderful for me, lighting me up inside like Mr. Watson's warmth or coloured fireworks. Unlike my father's frightening fire, mine was soft and joyous. Being part of a close-knit group made me realise my worth. Over time, I made more friends, laughed more, and my feelings swirled softly. Feeling "filled with fireworks" brought me immense happiness.

Being part of groups changed me. School and neighbourhood friends helped make my wish come true, making me feel like I belonged. The feeling was warm inside. I never heard anyone say, "We belong together," yet I felt it. Our games and the places we played created that sense. The environment told me: "You belong here." I realised that something within me made me feel that way. I was able to live my life where I belonged.

I realised belonging is internal while place is external. The sense inside tells me when I'm in the right place, an inner awareness showing both feeling and place.

That truth didn't save me for years, especially as a scared kid searching everywhere but inside myself. How could a child look inward for belonging when acceptance was outside, in groups, in games, in laughter? My insides screamed at me, loud, wild, relentless, yet I didn't know how to answer back or listen. All along, what I needed was already burning inside me, but fear kept my ears shut.

I learned that listening to my insides, even when it hurt, guided me towards true belonging. It is often hard to explain that life's most needed things, like belonging, are hidden inside us. For a traumatised child, it would have been easier if there had been signs showing where to belong, but there were none. I wished for a way to locate belonging, but I came to realise that the sign pointing the way was always inside me.

I first grasped the deep meaning of belonging around age nine. Debbie, my neighbour, stood out as the most beautiful girl in my world, as if she could be Miss Australia. She had shiny hair, a smile I could feel, and sparkling eyes. She looked just like a movie star to me. Time with Debbie felt effortless, a warm, fuzzy feeling I'd always longed for. I could call up that feeling anytime, anywhere, if I just remembered to. Laughter came easily.

Carol, my other favourite friend, felt almost like a sister, one who always made me laugh; we both had blonde, curly hair, and I delighted in that. Ann, another friend, came from up the hill to join us in the afternoons. Her black, wavy hair shimmered like satin, and I often wished for hair just like Ann's.

Living next door to a community hall was so much fun because the grounds became our playground. The yard was like one of those big backyards everyone wanted, so all the neighbourhood kids spent their afternoons together, riding bikes or climbing the hugest tree I have ever climbed. There were loads of kids in the grounds, and we always had the best time together.

After school, I spent more time with the neighbourhood kids. Brian and Billy rode their bikes every day, and I joined them. Slowly, I started feeling more alive and discovered joy and excitement within myself, gradually detaching from the storm at 1-5-8. Birthday party invitations began arriving, which amazed me. Did kids really like me? Did they see me? Maybe, just maybe, they did.

One hot summer Friday night, I attended a school friend's birthday party, and to my total surprise, I was allowed to go out alone. The party was about a twenty-minute run from my house, and I ran there and back on my own. I was overly excited to get out of my house that Friday night, no zsstt, no 6.30pm. Friday Fight Night in the kitchen around the dinner table.

As night fell, we played chase, catch, and kiss. The excitement was endless. I felt like the luckiest girl alive when the most beautiful boy, his long blonde hair flying, caught me and kissed me. Billy's eyes, as dark as midnight velvet, sparkled in the dim light. His gentle touch crept through my entire being; his quiet, powerful kiss was unlike anything I had ever known.

My puppy-love thoughts bounced like soft, blue-and-white bubbles, then soared from the rainbow's edge to the sun, past the purple sky. Everything sparkled in gorgeous madness. The feelings were the most profound and beautiful I had ever known. From then on, every abusive act by my father was less hurtful because when I left my body for a safer place up to the rainbow, away from my father's cruelty, I felt the safety and comfort of Billy. The memory of puppy love and the rainbow of comfort

stayed with me for many years, yet Billy never knew.
Thank goodness for that party and for Billy.

Many years later, I've come to realise that the experience
of puppy love truly matters. Those feelings lifted me
out of the numbness I had been living in, proving how
powerful genuine tenderness can be. For me, that moment
of kindness and gentle touch was life-saving. It taught me
not to underestimate the strength of a single moment of
tenderness for a child who has not experienced safety and
gentle touch.

Unsent Letter

Dear Feelings of Tenderness,

I waited for you to show yourselves to me.

Then you did!

$$-8-$$
My Jam

I recall my childhood vividly, and I was profoundly shaped by the dynamics of my family simply by being part of it. At the age of ten, I absorbed the many life skills needed to endure 1-5-8. One semi-dangerous skill I learned early in my school life was how to enter the locked house after school: a pseudo-burglar. It didn't feel right what I had to do to get inside the house, yet it was a simple fact. I needed to get inside the house, but it was locked up, and I had no key to open the door!

Our house sat on a flat area at the foot of a hill. It was low set and built on stumps, neither too high nor too low. The only way to enter the locked house was through a small, unlocked bathroom window, slightly ajar. There were, however, two obstacles to reaching that bathroom window and getting through it into the house! One was how to reach the unlocked window, and the second was how to get past the flaming-hot gas water tank directly underneath it.

It would have been a courageous leap from the ground directly to the windowsill, avoiding contact with the heated, lit gas tank; I never did try it in one flying leap. My approach was to carefully climb beside the burning-hot gas water tank cover, without burning myself or setting any clothes on fire. Then I tried to scale the heated cover and climb onto the windowsill safely, like something I once saw in the movies.

The first thing I did was lean as far as I could from the side steps onto the windowsill, which was ever so close but just out of reach. If I jumped to grab it, I risked brushing up against the hot-everything system, which I did most of the time. That burned my skin and hurt, yet I persisted, and eventually I became skilled at it. I learned that if I climbed onto the small unused stand on the ground, then climbed up the wall, I could hold onto the gas tank only for a moment at a time, so as not to burn my hand. I also learned to always carry a jumper in my school bag, which I'd use to cover my hands and protect them. I could then hold on and lift myself. I always brushed against the tank and always burned my arm too. I got stronger at lifting myself over the wall onto the windowsill, and although it wasn't easy, I got better at it.

Risk-taking became my jam, and not just as a burglar but while learning greater skills from the theatrics of life at 1-5-8.

I wonder why I never had a key to getting inside?

It was just the way it was!

Having figured out how to survive inside my house, I also learned how to get into a locked house, burglar-style, which added to my growing list of survival techniques.

-9-
The Smile Factory

I wore the secret dysfunction in my family like an oversized, heavy, prickly coat I could not seem to take off. I was a young girl in a battling suburban family with a secret ambition. This was established early in my life: to rescue my worn-out, severely beaten mother from my father's aggressions and his perfected backhand.

I dreaded the chaos in the house, but the silence terrified me even more. Silence too long or too often meant something terrible was brewing, like a witch's cauldron beginning to bubble. I could never tell whether what I felt was fear of my father or grief for not having the kind, loving father I'd dreamed of. Could it be both? I was confused. I never knew grief could feel so much like fear. Even when I wasn't actively afraid, the feeling stayed the same: a flutter in my chest and a restless, uncomfortable hum inside my body. Other times, I felt as if I didn't make sense at all, as if I'd had one too many drinks, like my mother did, or as if I were a bit dazed, the way I felt after my father backhanded me across the head.

But, somewhere deep inside, a thought would surface: I don't mind that much because he won't be with me for my whole life. It was a strange sort of comfort. I couldn't wait for the time when I would live in a world without his destructive behaviours.

One sunny afternoon, I was sitting, thinking about my father once again, as I too often did, when the squeak of the nearby neighbours' swings and the high-pitched giggles of the owners riding them drifted over, filling me with warmth and longing. Their life was my dream.

In the evenings, the light from their windows spilled peace and calm across the fence. I wonder if they felt happy together in their home?

The lights in our house told a different story.

My life was not full of joy-filled giggles and squeaky swings. Living felt heavy in my body, with a nausea that rolled through my insides and sometimes spilled out, as though the sickness in me might be visible. I knew what it looked like when someone's insides showed on the outside; my father's fury was written all over his face: the thunder, the clenched jaw, the mad rumbling inside him spilling out in every space claimed.

One afternoon, while sucking the sweet honey from my friends, the nasturtiums, a question flooded my mind. Could people see my insides on my outsides, the way I could see my father's?

The thought made me nervous enough to walk to the bathroom, where the only mirror hung.

I was frightened of what I might see. My insides felt warped, out of shape. I leaned in close, staring for a long time. What did swirling insides look like on a face? What did a brain not working properly look like?

I did not see a "dirty-rotten-mongrel-bastard-kid" staring back. That's who my father saw, but I didn't. I didn't see angry eyes or a clenched jaw. I saw a curious girl, searching thoroughly for an answer.

She had dark circles under dull eyes and gloom on her unsmiling face, the same sadness I recognised in my mother's. I at once noticed my face did not smile easily. When I tried it, it felt odd, like wearing pyjamas made of steel. It was stiff, fake, manufactured, like something made in a smile factory.

The muscles around my mouth strained to shape themselves into the upward curve. It felt peculiar. I realised I had never thought about smiling as something that needed practice.

So, I started secretly training. Day after day, staring into the mirror, I taught my face to smile. Eventually, I raised my eyebrows, and suddenly the whole thing felt better, like the perfect blend of happiness. I was so relieved I didn't look like my father in the face, even when I felt as angry as he was.

I could hide my insides on my outside. My face, my being, was nothing like my father's. My pretending to smile, to be happy, worked, at least for a while. The project was a complete success.

But success came with a side effect: I became even more curious. If I could make myself look like a normal girl, could I act like one, too? Could people see through my deliberateness, lack of trust, shyness, and the sorrow buried deep inside me?

The question followed me when I was riding my bike with friends, patting the barky dogs two doors up, or shouting back at Janet from school.

Lying on my bed one afternoon, halfway through listing a new "obsession plan," I stopped. I wasn't about to do one more obsessive thing. No more trying to fix my father's temper, my mother's meanness, or me, the kid who wasn't good at anything. Apparently!

The whole obsession with obsession was consuming me. I knew then that it was not just habits, but fear. Fear ruled every choice I made, and that feeling stayed with me well into adulthood.

Even as an adult, I questioned everything about myself. I did not know how to act appropriately, who I was meant to be, the same as the others in my family, or how I was meant to feel about life inside 1-5-8. Maybe the confusion about myself was born from the frequent confusion of mind at 1-5-8; one minute my mother was handing my father the belt to thrash me, the next she would make me a meal like it was an act of love; one afternoon, my father would choke me with soap, and the next he would buy me the best softball glove he could afford.

Although I cannot remember exactly when, I gave up the things I wanted, wished for, or needed in exchange for peace inside. I chose irrelevance to live the life of the unseen child, invisible and inconsequential. Safer.

I kept quiet in groups at times, then became less calm as I got to know the new friends better, which worked well enough when needed. At home, staying small kept me safe. At school, it kept me out of trouble, except for the occasional blow-ups with Janet, my school friend. Janet was really smart, smarter than me, because she always got the right answers to the math questions. I didn't! I really don't know exactly why Janet and I didn't like each other, but it was true. We just didn't. But I wanted to be smart like Janet. I so wanted that.

I was good at other things. Like reading invisible things; tension, safety, and danger in every room. I often felt the fear of what I actually wanted while the same fear told me not to want it. If a teacher or another adult came into our classroom, I felt okay because I trusted them, and since Mr. Watson knew them, it felt safe for me. But sometimes the teachers who also knew Mr. Watson weren't as kind as he was, and I learned that too. When other teachers were on playground duty, they sometimes behaved brashly and meanly, raising their voices at students like my father, so I grew fearful. They were teachers like Mr. Watson, but I didn't feel safe with them. Mr. Watson was my touch tree.

Naiveté in human behaviour, I have since learned, can be a beautiful thing. In childhood, it saved my life. I thought everyone who was loud and mean was just like my father yet they weren't.

Experiencing the opportunity to explore so many different feelings as a child felt heavy then. Not ideal, yet I learned many other things from those big, frightening feelings and circumstances. I experienced a quirky sense of the absurd amid those heavy emotions and crazy goings-on inside 1-5-8, which eventually lightened my mood and made me laugh. Eventually being the operative word.

The gift of that sense of the absurd brought to my life a sense of humour, dark and witty, that is unparalleled by any other expression I ever learned.

Amid the chaos of childhood, I initially mistook my sadness for tiredness. I felt guilty for wanting more than nothing, because nothing was precisely what my father told me I deserved. I lived in self-denial, as did the family. I do not know whether I chose to believe my parents' version of me or whether fear did the choosing, but either way, I followed. I had no options.

I did not know I was allowed to take up space in my kitchen, or that it was okay to be in my kitchen expecting peace, free from hidings. I did not know I was allowed to speak up to angry adults abusing me. I did not know a million other things about myself or my life, and that ignorance born in 1-5-8 would steer me into many unsafe situations to come.

Unsent Letter

Dear Me,

I love your curiosity.

Hold it safely, Little One.

– 10 –

The Thief Who Wasn't

Late November, aged twelve, I was almost finished packing my holiday bag in my bedroom. I was excited because on Monday morning, I was going to the end-of-year school camp about two hours away. There, we would swim in the still waters of a crystal-clear creek.

Over 100 primary school kids from all over Brisbane were due to arrive at the school camp at the same time.

I was excited about spending five days away from home, free. No thunder, just me in my own camp school hut with friends from my school and new friends from other schools.

We listened for our names to be called by a teacher, after which we were shown to our neat hut, our accommodation for the week. Most of the girls I shared the hut with were chatty, so I felt like I belonged immediately.

A girl named Bonnie, with a high blonde ponytail that bounced with her every movement, talked to me as I unpacked my bag. Bonnie's bed, opposite mine, was already messed up as she jumped onto it, wriggling in glee.

She knew other girls in the hut as they called out her name, laughing at her antics. Bonnie easily made her school friends giggle, especially with her loud storytelling about what she had packed for camp.

"Here they…are," she shouted, "my snorkel and goggles," as she tried to drag them over her high, bouncy pigtail. Bonnie was brash and funny, and I was already glad my new friend was in the same hut as me.

The next morning, everyone at the camp had breakfast together. The long wooden benches were the same length as the tables. We were squished together on the seats, and we didn't mind at all.

After cleaning up, we marched in two lines to the oval for a game's tournament. In teams, we played Red Rover, Red Light, Green Light, Dodge the Ball, and Mini Soccer. We used hula hoops to jump through, spin on, and hop into, one after the other, like hopscotch. Tunnel Ball was the last game we played on the green oval in the beaming sun. Then we quickly changed into our togs, grabbed our beach towels and swam in the clear, still waters of the wide creek.

Lunch was in the same outdoor area as breakfast, and then we headed back to the oval for more games and physical activities that lasted well into the afternoon. We ran, crawled, jumped, ducked, and danced. There were cartwheels and handstands with smiles and giggles at the fun of that afternoon.

We hung out in our groups from the first day, chatting the whole time. I knew from that first fun day that this entire week of school camp was going to be unreal.

The next most enjoyable aspect was meeting everyone in the outdoor dining precinct for meals.

Everyone was in the same place at the same time: teachers, kids, and camp staff. The noise at mealtimes was almost deafening until the teachers called for us to tone it down. At the end of meals, each long table was packed with kids lining up to wash and dry dishes before playing word games, rapid-fire style.

On the second night, after dinner, we returned to our seats, having washed and dried our plates. During the noisy, almost deafening period, an announcement from a loudspeaker drifted across the dining precinct. "Quiet, students, quiet please!"

This took some time.

All was finally quiet, with all attention on the teacher holding the speaker in his hand.

Two words came out of the loudspeaker.

My name.

The teacher went on, "Please stand on your seat, young lady."

Kids looked around at each other, probably searching for the person with that name. Not everyone knew me, so the chatting began again as they waited for me to stand on my seat. The teacher reminded the group again that he expected quiet.

I was scared because I didn't understand or know why!

Awkwardly and slowly, I climbed to stand on my seat. I did as I was told, always. Then the voice rang out again. "This girl is a thief; she stole a pair of earrings from another girl in her hut."

"Huh," rang out for a long time from the audience, seemingly shocked, though not as amazed as I was.

I shook my head. Earrings? What? Me? No! I looked down at my friends seated at their places, noticing the raised eyebrows and snarky looks on their faces.

I was mortified, embarrassed, and humiliated.

"Remember this girl's face and her name," the teacher said, stating his assumptions out loud. He spelled out my guilt to the entire group.

"Ooh-arr," the next mass sound, more disapproving of me.

I held my breath. Gutted.

The last word game of the evening did not include me. I was to stand beside the other teachers.

I was a thief with a face and name to remember.

I felt like I was back at 1-5-8, being blamed again for something I had not done.

The school kids were then dismissed.

Not me. I was told to stay behind to answer questions about the earrings.

Why, how, and when? What made me steal a pair of earrings?

I stood alone with the two male teachers facing me as I told them, through tears and sobs, it was not me. I did not steal anyone's earrings.

They stared at me for as long as I gave my "statement".

Then silence.

My words and expressions of innocence were a waste of time, as they already believed I was the thief.

The first time I heard about the stolen earrings was when everyone else did, after dinner. If something like that had happened at school, a teacher would have first asked if I was the one who did the thing I was being accused of. Even if I had done it, I would never have been made a spectacle of. If a kid got into a fight or kicked a football through a teacher's car windscreen (sorry, Mr. Watson), they were never made to stand on parade in front of all students and teachers to be humiliated. I wondered if the teacher who told me to stand on my chair was like my father, which really upset me as I worried about what could happen to me next. Mr. Watson would never have permitted that kind of persecution and humiliation.

I had never seen a student publicly humiliated before. I did not like it at all. The cold sensation made me realise that something was off.

Yet this had just happened to me. It was the most "unbelonging" feeling I could have, and I felt "un-friended" and untrusted in those moments.

First, I did not steal the earrings or sneak into the hut alone. Second, the earrings were for pierced ears, which I didn't have. Why would I want earrings for pierced ears? I tried to tell the teachers that I did not steal the earrings and showed them that I did not have pierced ears. I was not heard. I was sent back to my hut alone, feeling disgraced in my humiliation.

Bloody-Dirty-Rotten-Mongrel-Bastards!

Debilitating shame from the misguided blame lived inside me until the end of year seven school camp.

For the remaining days of camp, I felt embarrassed. I was ignored by most of the girls in my hut and ridiculed by other kids.

Two days later, Bonnie snarled and yelled at me for stealing her earrings. She spun on her heels and left the hut. I followed her, calling out, "It was not me, Bonnie. It wasn't. I did not take your earrings."

Because I did not.

It was Bonnie, the fun girl in my hut. She was the girl whose earrings were stolen. The teachers did not tell anyone that.

I was convinced Bonnie knew I hadn't taken her earrings, just as I knew I hadn't. I genuinely felt like an outcast at camp.

I was a dirty-rotten-mongrel-bastard!

Those last two days were brutal. I was not invited to join teams and was instead seated on the sideline under the watch of teachers. I felt like I was on one of those big advertising boards on the highways. The thing standing out, the thing you look at. That was me. The thing that stood out. The thing they looked at.

Thank goodness the last night of camp finally arrived, as I could not wait to get back to my house, the disasters of 1-5-8. At least I knew what to expect there, which was better than being in a place where I felt alone and was treated like a thief.

At dinner that evening, a girl named Anne came to tell me she believed I did not steal Bonnie's earrings. A moment later, the teacher with the loudspeaker, who had been speaking that terrible night I was accused of theft, stood behind me, asking me to stand up again.

"Oh god, what now?"

His words echoed inside my head as he told me that Bonnie had admitted to making up the story about her earrings being stolen. They were never stolen; it was a lie. And I had been burdened with the blame, standing on the bench seat for the whole school camp population to witness, to remember my face and my name.

The teacher left, and I sat looking downwards, silent for a long time. At some point, I felt relieved and looked at Anne. We said nothing, perhaps still shocked.

Over the years, I have often wondered about the depth of the agony within me due to the repercussions of being wrongly accused of theft. I felt those same feelings when I reflected upon my school camp.

Were there any repercussions for the teachers, the blamers who got it wrong and believed Bonnie's fanciful story and not my truth?

There was not one "sorry we got it wrong" from anyone in authority at the camp. Not from any of the teachers who made the announcement, who named, blamed, and shamed me. Nor from the teachers who kept me back that evening to ask about the earrings, who did not listen to or believe me; nor were they sorry for setting me aside from activities for being a 'known thief'.

No one took the time to check on me for those two days and nights. Nor did they meet their obligation to care for me or talk to me about how I felt living with the humiliation.

And there was no announcement to the masses that I was not a thief, nor was there any announcement to everyone that the story was a fabrication. So, everyone at camp still believed I was the thief, including the kids at my school, whom I would see next week. It took me some time to feel the feelings of being believed after all.

Knowing I was now believed did not erase the impact on me and my life. The feeling of not being believed remained in my body. When I let my parents know what had happened to me, I felt on the inside like they thought it was no big deal. I was ignored.

They did not have my back. They ignored my sadness and humiliation. No enquiry was made to my teacher, who did not attend the camp. No complaint was made on my behalf after I told them about the lies and embarrassment I faced. Did I really expect anything more from them?

The impact of not being believed had already taken root in me, fuelled by my previous efforts to plead with my parents to believe me. The label of liar instilled in me such fear that I would blame myself for things I hadn't done.

I often wonder if those same burning questions live inside others who are victims of misplaced blame and have faced ridicule without a voice or advocate. Those moments changed my ability to trust forever.

Unsent Letter

Dear Bonnie,

I hope I never ever

See you again,

Because your behaviours remind me

Of you know who!

-11-
Unbelievable Me

The new year arrived quickly, and my mother informed me I would be packing for a beachside holiday with people I barely knew - again, getting rid of their kid. No surprise there. This had become my parents' routine: sending their daughter on trips with their friends, not with my friends, whom I knew.

I've always felt like a burden to my parents, and now, more than ever, to this family during our beach holiday. This tradition of my parents freeing themselves from the burden of having me continued at the expense of my wants, needs for safety, and my well-being.

Holidaying with this family was ultra uncomfortable because the two boys, who were a few years older than me, were difficult to get along with. One was the son, and the other was his friend. I was still twelve. These teenagers were two smart-mouthed boys to the adults and even more smart-mouthed towards me.

The first night, I slept little, wondering how I would get through the week with these two tricky boys.

While I was making my breakfast toast, the mother came into the kitchen. I could see she was angry from her expression as she began questioning the three of us about the money missing from her wallet. No one owned up to it, including me, since I hadn't taken the money. There was a lot of investigation into who had been in or near her bedroom, where her handbag containing the wallet was kept, and who knew that. She questioned each of us at the breakfast bar, telling us how disgusted she was with whoever had taken her money, when, and how, even? With the investigation complete and no eyewitnesses or bystanders coming forwards, only one person could have been a suspect, despite being with the others the entire day before.

"It wasn't me," said both teenage boys.

"Well, it wasn't me," I spoke up quickly.

The mother was even more angry by then.

"Well, someone is lying, aren't they?" she shouted as she walked out of the kitchen.

All was quiet for a short period of time until the angry mother returned.

"You," she said, pointing to me. "Pack your stuff, you're leaving now."

The thief! The stealer of the money, the twenty dollars, was me!

I did not react. I had nothing inside of me to react. I was the girl not to be believed.

I, as a girl, a person, was not believable; I was an unbelievable person.

After being given a dressing-down by both the holidaymaker parents, I was packed into the family car by the angry, appalled mother and driven back to my house in Brisbane. It was a silent car ride, seated in the back, feeling nauseous the whole hour-long drive, knowing I had not stolen the money and what awaited my arrival. Once again, a nobody, a nothingness, just a breathing body, an unheard being.

Embarrassment and fear stifled me as I walked, step by step, into my house, waiting for the outrage to begin. But first, I, along with both my parents, was forced to hear the story of the stolen money. The appalled, angry mother cried as she recounted how disgusted and shocked she felt, given all she had done for me, taking me on her vacation and trusting me! She never wanted to see my face again! Both parents remained silent as she made her point, then watched her storm off to her car. The car screeched off, tires squealing. It was quite a performance.

Then the Theatrics of 1-5-8 opened in chaos...

My father's eyes glared at mine with the madness I had anticipated, and my mother turned and walked away, into the kitchen.

Zsstt...

Grabbing my arm, hard, my father dragged me to my bedroom. Pulling my packed holiday bag from my shoulder, he threw it, then me onto the floor. He was seething!

"You, dirty-rotten-little-mongrel-bastard-of-a-germ. We sent you on a holiday, and you stole money. How dare you?"

As he came at me, with a raised hand, I climbed to my feet. He then landed his professional-style backhand on me. Not the best he had ever thrown, as I fell onto the end of my bed this time, not with the full force of his swing at me, but in anticipation of it.

He came at me, grabbing my shoulders to make me stand. I pulled away, walking backwards. Then stopped as I was cornered.

I stood tall, feet apart, staring at him. I do not know where the strength came from, but I felt strong to my bones.

I screamed back, one syllable, one breath, just like he did,

"I-did-not-take-the-money. I would not take money!"

"You did, you-thieved-it," he yelled into my face as he raised his hand once again.

I raised my arm to block the swing at me, stopping his hand from hitting my face, but this time, his strength was too much.

He hit my arm away, smacking my forehead, then hit me again with the other hand. I flew onto the floor as I covered my face with my arms. He stood over me, throwing all the words he could find to belittle me.

"Don't-you-ever-think-I-will-forget-what-you-did-you-thieving-rotten-little-germ-of-a-thing."

He stormed out, and I crawled back onto my bed and lay there for the rest of the day.

I wanted to unappoint my father as my father. Birth fathers wished to believe their kids, didn't they? I wanted a father like that, someone who believed me when I told him stuff.

Recovery from his beatings took days, sometimes weeks, and the emotional grief took years to accept, in some small way, if at all. The bruising and throbbing in my limbs from a more brutal hiding made it harder to move quickly or normally.

It was worse in winter, as my body felt the painful strikes more acutely in the colder weather.

I knew the bruises, aches, soreness, and tears on my body were there for absolutely no reason, not because I had done anything wrong, but because my father never believed me. That made me feel all that much worse, so much worse.

...and four weeks later, my mother told me that the son's friend, the smart-mouthed teenager, had taken the money!

My father did not say sorry. He did not say sorry!

Did I expect him to come to me to say, "I should have asked you about the stolen money before backhanding you, four times!"

Nor did he apologise for smacking me. I never heard one sorry word from my father or my mother for blaming me for stealing the money I did not steal.

I am still awaiting the apology from the appalled, appalling mother as well.

With hatred I could not explain, I hated my father. I wanted to create longer, more innovative words that were more meaningful than "hate," since it wasn't strong enough to capture how I felt about him. I wished he would die.

Not die in a horrible way, but die like go away forever, be gone from my life forever, somehow just not be there ever again.

Nobody, not one person, offered a sincere apology for subjecting me to such humiliation and savagery. No, that did not happen to me! I was a traumatised child, inconsequential, obscure, and the scapegoat for many, it seemed.

I grew up voiceless amid the many conflicts at 1-5-8, unsure exactly how I could be heard and how I would be heard.

Had my face, my body language, become that of a victim? Both must have shown on me and in me, as this is the only thing that would make sense for being blamed for things I did not do.

What I had to say to adults in my life seemed of no value, no importance.

That had become evident, no question.

The lack of validation for those critical issues has had a profoundly damaging impact on my self-worth, a process that has taken tens of years to understand and regenerate.

My parents never acknowledged any of my beatings, the pain, bruising, cuts, or swelling they caused, nor comforted me in my mental anguish, ever.

The fact that my parents never discussed my agony of not being believed, nor gave me validation for being cleared of the offences, nor suffering the pointless flogging, saw me sustain the most hurt of all. I wish they had talked it out with me, acknowledging my honesty as their kid, rather than the thief they were told I was.

I did not know if my mother ever told my father I was not the thief, that I didn't steal the earrings or the money, because I noticed my father became angrier with me more often.

I became less interested in more things. My self-care mattered less to me; my life no longer seemed worth living. My body was in pain every day. I felt nauseous every day, I feared my father every day. I feared the 6.30 pm dinner table stalking every day even more than I had before. I could see no reason I wanted or needed to stay alive to live in my life in my house and with my family.

I wanted and needed all my inside pain to stop. Forever.

I felt embarrassed about showing up every morning to see my family, as I felt like I was in the way when I heard my parents looking for the next place or family to send me to for school holidays. More strangers to holiday with! I never wanted to go with another unknown family, knowing they probably didn't want me either. But I was sent, and I went.

Would I be blamed yet again for stealing something? Would I get a flogging when I arrived home? Was my life worth living? This question bothered me more often.

Unsent Letter

Dear Parents

Why did you want to be parents

or, did you?

-12 -
At 6.30pm

By the age of eleven, I had almost mastered ways to deflect my father's attention at dinnertime. I was taller, stronger, and cleverer now because I couldn't be anything else if I wanted to stay upright. Survival depended on being more imaginative, smarter, and a faster runner, which made me a successful escapee at times. I became the family's entertainer, crafting performances around the small, red-and-white-flecked Laminex table in our square kitchen.

And I always felt scared at 6.30pm.

6.15pm: I checked on my breathing, taking big breaths in and slowly out.

6.28pm: Time. I stood tall. I could do this.

6.29pm: The call to the dinner table landed unexpectedly, one minute early.

6.30pm: I slowly lit up inside. I felt brave. Another performance! I would do this to the best of my ability, with my wit and highly crafted imagination developed during the theatrics at 1-5-8. I was what this family needed!

I aimed to replace the chaos of dinnertime fears with a more meaningful, enjoyable, and relaxed family dining experience. The family would gather at 6.30pm with me, the entertainer, centre stage. I would take them into safety at mealtimes, and dinner would be a time when I had never felt better.

Yes, the dirty-rotten-mongrel-bastard-kid was now in charge!

At precisely 6.30 and eleven seconds, I arrived at the smallish, red-and-white-flecked, rectangular Laminex dinner table, still feeling, unsurprisingly, scared. The Laminex table in the kitchen reminded me that the best thing about this unwelcoming nightly jaunt was the chance to bring a welcoming performance with me. The Dining Entertainment!

I took my seat, nervously excited.

The food on its way, in all its gloriousness, felt as if it was being personally delivered by Mao Tse-tung himself because my father was a communist.

My father grew our vegetables with his own hands, taking genuine pride in providing this gold-like sustenance for us, or so he said. He told us he would ensure every single piece of his homegrown fare was appreciated. "No waste," he reminds us regularly.

I felt the weight of those words every single day at 6.30pm. How could I forget, with the meals routinely featuring meat and what looked like twenty-six vegetables and gravy? My mother's creative cooking was always beautifully presented and tasty, but she served us huge, overgenerous portions. Urgh! My father's huge appetite dictated the supersized helpings, I think! Alternatively, she may have done so out of love for him and for her role in our family. I still reckoned the meals were stupid-sized.

Sitting at the kitchen table, I lost my confidence and felt sick. I tried to settle my insides, as this was the closest we came to one another every day, for approximately thirty minutes each evening. I detested being that close to my parents, feeling like I was on the brink of conflict, waiting for it to erupt at any moment.

6.34pm: Breathe, sit still. I was ready to go, prepared to eat. "Thank you," I said to my mother as I analysed the stupid-sized meal placed in front of me.

I felt scared when I see that heaped dinner plate, for so many reasons. I heard once that we eat with our eyes, so I used mine to decide what looked good and what I could eat. What could I actually swallow?

There are many places where I can eat, and in each, I see and feel differently. Eating in the kitchen at 6.30pm, I felt sick every time. It was a strange feeling about food, because I could enjoy dinner at my cousin's house; I liked the food and the conversation. But not in that kitchen, which is one reason I felt scared at 6.30pm, under pressure to eat dinner at 1-5-8.

I knew exactly what I must eat, and it's not going to be fun because I was fully aware of what happened when I didn't eat the food served to me in that kitchen! My eyes didn't like what they saw on my dinner plate, and I could almost hear the potential explosive detonation from my father if I didn't eat this oversized "father-portion" meal.

6.34 and thirty seconds: I began the dining-entertainment experiment. I loved my secret of rearranging the food on my dinner plate so it wouldn't attract my father's attention. I felt so bloody clever! I would be in big trouble if he noticed! He would say I was playing with my food, which I was, but not really! I was simply, genuinely, trying to make it look like I could stomach it.

The slow shifting of food around my plate soothed my simmering nervous system, and I felt better about eating at least some of it. I slid the vegetables, peas, carrots, corn, zucchini, and choko, cooked with their prickly skins on, to one side of my plate, then moved the potato and pumpkin to another area. Mother poured the gravy directly onto the potato and pumpkin. Then I began the eating part. The act of moving my food around was necessary because it gave me time to read the mood at the dinner table. I got time to analyse my feelings and nerves. Was my stomach swirling? Was my throat tightening, or was I relaxed enough to put food into my mouth, to both chew and swallow it?

This was my moment. My theatre was now open. It was where my storytelling came to life for my audience. Nervously, I created stories using cutlery and salt-and-pepper shakers, then, eventually, my food as characters in the tales. I kept my family laughing all the while leaving no room for the face of fury to interrupt the goings on of the tall tale.

The other main aim of the dinner entertainment was to ensure I pleased my father by praising his hand-raised foods.

"Oh, Dad, this pumpkin is so orange, so delicious. You have done a fantastic job growing this one. The zucchini is so fresh, green, and tasty."

I delivered those words with an emptiness of sorts. I appreciated how my parents fed me, yet chose my words carefully so as not to say too much, which was risky; my father was too "slap happy" around me.

I didn't care enough about the food to praise my father excessively, but I did so without prompting.

I ate a little of the meal and liked some of it, but I only ate it to get to the dessert. There were deals to be negotiated to get dessert in front of me.

I, however, decided eventually that I wanted nothing to do with deals to get to the dessert. I was happy not to eat dinner and go to bed hungry, since it wasn't a real deal anyway. Whenever I chose that option, my parents never let me go to bed hungry; I was forced to eat dinner. Urgh! Yes, mealtimes meant deals, threats, forced solutions, and one more disagreement in a lengthy list of pointless disputes.

6.47 and I was again, for yet another night, trying to avoid all deals at "Fight Nights" in the kitchen.

"How many peas did you give me tonight, Mum?" I asked, playfully.

She smiled.

"Let me begin the pea count! Tonight, I will count in fives!" I looked amusingly at my plate; my little finger held against my lips!

"Five, ten," I said, using my fork to spin the peas into small pods to be sure I got the pea count exactly right.

"Twenty, twenty-five, thirty."

"You missed one," my mother pointed out, "over there, under the potato!"

"I guess I will just have to start again." I smiled at the thought that I, the kid, was holding centre stage, raising laughs from the entire kitchen table audience.

Relief! Sheer Relief!

"Five, ten, fifteen, twenty," as I moved those little green things around my plate, under the potato and over the pumpkin, sliding corn down the gravy, making up another laughable story of shy peas while continuing to use my food as props!

"Mr. Pepper and Mrs. Salt-Shaker are worried about their peas! Why so shy? Whatever could be the matter with our shy little peas?"

I adored the storytelling at dinner time more than I thought I would. My anxieties defused in a small way. The ongoing laughter and giggles told me my story was appreciated, too.

I felt joy inside, and my smile was big that night. But I could also feel my father's eyes on me: the usual 6.30pm stuff, his ritual of watching me and stalking me. I spooned one heaped spoonful of pumpkin into my mouth, chewed a little, then swallowed. He diverted his full attention elsewhere. Phew!

6.51: Both parents giggled about something I said, gobbled their meals, and then scraped their plates, depositing the scraps into the bin.

How did anyone eat all that food so quickly? Urgh.

My mother rinsed plates, cooking pots, and pans, then went to the fridge.

It was 6.56pm.

Then,

Zsstt…

One crack of a bottle of beer, which I would pay for, pay for his hatred of alcohol-fuelled people. My mother took her beer and cigarettes to the back steps.

Oh no. My eyes shifted to my father. His eyes glared at my mother walking past him, then turned to stare right through me.

Those very eyes tracked every inch of my large, piled dinner plate. Looking down at it too, I felt my throat tighten with fear. His eyes of steel made my sick stomach want to heave.

My mind kept telling me I had to, that I was required to, eat everything on the dinner plate. My insides began shaking.

6.59pm: My father and I were in the kitchen alone.

I stared at my dinner plate. I could hear his feet on the lino flooring, pacing back and forth, to the ABC news broadcasting in the lounge room, then back to me, analysing both, I reckoned.

"Eat the food on your plate, and then you can go to the TV," said my father carelessly as he walked up the hallway into the lounge room.

I tried to eat some more of my dinner, something soft. Potatoes were always good.

After a brief time, he returned, leaning close to my dinner plate. "Open your mouth, you imbecile. Eat!"

He was angry with his whole face now, not just his eyes. His jaw was clenched, his lips were tighter, and he was breathing more heavily.

He was on his way to hitting me. I could feel it.

I shoved a whole fork filled with potato into my mouth and spoke through a filled mouth, "Mm, trying. Mm, trying!"

His face came closer to mine, eyes boring holes into mine.

The whole of me felt so sick, I thought I might vomit in his face if he came close again.

"Eat. Try harder. You will sit here until you eat every skerrick of the food I grew for you, you wasteful-little-mongrel-bastard."

I was chewing quickly; he was yelling fast. And loud!

7.04 pm: His face became redder and redder as it closed in on mine; he smelt like wood shavings!

He continued his red-faced, clenched-teeth, steely-eyed rage in my face.

I nodded my head as I had the maximum amount of food in my mouth. I could not say, "I am trying to eat, Dad, I am trying," but my nod was saying it.

Nervously trying to swallow, I gagged on a heaped mouthful of his golden sustenance.

I was ignored.

I felt guilty as I thought he thought I was pretending. I tried to eat one piece of roast beef, chewing and chewing and chewing that one piece of meat I had managed to put into my mouth. It just would not break down; no matter how long I chewed it, I couldn't swallow it, and I couldn't take it out of my mouth. He would shove it back in if I did.

Pacing around the kitchen table, watching me, he grew more agitated, and I grew more restless. Losing his stance, he eventually slumped onto the seat beside me.

I stop breathing. His body stiffened. My body stilled, petrified, unable to move.

"You rotten little bastard," he spat at me angrily.

He demanded that I eat his homegrown food. The words were growing louder with my every failing effort. Terrified, I slowly leaned away from him, but he leaned into me, then slowly got to his feet, stood over me, and forced food into my mouth with my fork. I couldn't open my mouth; I was frozen. He pushed the fork into my mouth and hurt my lips. I pulled away.

7.10pm: The fork flew across the kitchen. He lost his fight with his own temper.

I felt my body leaving the kitchen. I was going somewhere over the rainbow, way up high, where I was safe.

Unexpectedly, I felt the thrust of his grabbing hand on the back of my neck, then one around my hair, lifting me from my seat, marching me down the hallway until we reached the bathroom.

One hand still tightly holding my hair, he pushed my head into the bathroom sink with the other, screaming at me, words I couldn't make out.

I screamed, "No!" Or tried to.

I tried to push his hand away, but couldn't. He held my head down. His weapon appeared in my face; he pushed the cake of soap in his hand into my mouth until I gagged. He continued to push it further in, trying to rub it along my teeth, his strong arms holding me still.

"You dirty-rotten-mongrel-bastard, you-wasteful-little-mongrel-bastard."

I couldn't breathe with my mouth and throat filled with a solid cake of soap. I tried to scream the scream I wanted to scream, but it would not come out. The struggle between my father and me went on for a long time; the bruising hold was tight, the pushing and gagging longer than the time I needed to draw breath. My body felt heavy, my mind darkened in the bathroom light, and my breath failed to reach my lungs. I never could tell how long the push and shove lasted on any given occasion, but when I opened my eyes, he was not there. He was never there. And neither was she.

I lay on the floor, nauseated, continuing to gag and eventually vomiting. I didn't know what time it was.

I drew deep breaths through my nose, filling my lungs, until I began to breathe slowly and more easily. I raised my arm towards the bathroom sink, pulling myself up from the floor. Slowly, I stumbled to my feet and stared at the cake of soap near the tap. I could see teeth marks in the slimy, yellow, creamy substance. Tears came easily as I gagged into the sink. I looked up, and the bathroom mirror reflected the whole story, transcribed on my face:

one more defeat at the hands of the fury, one more scar on the soul of this girl, the clever little entertainer who tried but lost.

I continued to look at the face in the mirror. I had tried so hard to save myself from him. Yet I failed, again.

I loved that face in the mirror.

I bloody loved that brave little kid.

I quietly tiptoed her to bed. At least in the aftermath, she was safe for a while.

Unsent Letter

Dear Meanest Father,

What made you use a cake of soap

to choke me with?

Did it happen to you

as a kid?

-13-

The Follow Up Game

My father always captained a follow-up game the morning after my severe reprimands. As a keen athlete, I spent the summer months training at the not-so-local outdoor pool. I usually caught the train there at about 5am, then took a couple of buses to school.

The follow-up game, however, slightly altered my usual training morning routine. The game was always the same and involved my father's specialty homemade cocktail, which he called Tiger's Milk.

That morning, still tasting soap and still feeling sick, my father woke me at 4.30am with his big, fake smile. He told me he had made me a special breakfast. His hand held the Tiger's Milk, which he passed to me as I lay in my bed, still waking up.

The Tiger's Milk, his favourite breakfast, was a horrible-tasting concoction of two raw eggs, one cup of whole cream milk, and two tablespoons of malted milk powder, shaken by his own hands for approximately three minutes.

It was now in my hands, to drink right then, right in front of him.

76

"It will make you swim faster," he laughed.

He disgusted me as much as the drink did.

I wanted to tell him that Tiger's Milk needed a rename, mate, let's come up with a new one.

"I feel guilty for making you black out last night, so I got up early and made you my favourite drink. Come on, drink it, so I do not feel so bad."

He does have some awareness of his madness after the fact! It seems.

As always, I drank at least one mouthful; it always made me feel sick, yet I did it, knowing it would keep him happy for a time.

His ritual, his madness, and his projecting his loathing of my mother's drinking onto me continued. A complex cocktail of fear, loyalty, and anger kept me silently compliant. There was a fear of his wrath, misplaced loyalty to maintain the peace, and simmering anger at being trapped in that cycle. These conflicting feelings bound me to continuing this forced morning ritual.

Did my father compound his fury over his wife's use of alcohol with fury over his daughter's lack of respect for his providing her food, to justify feeding her soap as punishment?

Would I ever find out?

Unsent Letter

Dear Mean Father,

Tell me, what makes you hit me

when my mother drinks beer?

Can you help me understand?

-14-

Sporting Minds

The sickly-sweet taste of Tiger's Milk lingered in my mouth long after that 4.30am ritual. It was thick, tasting disgusting, pulling my stomach into knots. My body, still reeling from the past night's chaos, moved through the day as if weighed down by invisible chains. Even as I boarded trains and buses to swim, the echoes of my father's 6.30pm surveillance of me and the 'father impersonator' haunted me.

My muscles were strong from training, and by the time I reached the pool, my lungs were ready to inhale freedom, but my body already carried residual tension, nausea, fatigue, and the certainty that I had failed again. I learned early that the mental abuse of home did not end at the dinner table or in my bedroom. It travelled with me, infiltrating every step, breath, and action.

Yet sport was my sanctuary. My one place where I could attempt to outrun that weight, if only for a few hours. When I entered the water or swung the bat, I felt a fleeting sense of relief. And so, I tried.

Softball was a release. The crack of the bat. The hiss of the ball. Muscles tensed, poised. Ready. Yet, even there, home's shadow lingered, its presence inescapable. I felt the grip of past echoes, the reminders of chaos. I yearned

79

to break free. To swing with reckless abandon. To feel the surge of adrenaline without the weight of haunting thoughts.

The upper body strength I had from swimming should have been enough. My arm could throw a ball easily. My legs could run fast. But when my mind filled with the echoes of my father's words, useless-hopeless-dirty-rotten-mongrel-bastard, my body betrayed me.

Training sessions were meant to release energy, tension, and fear. Sometimes, my muscles tightened. My chest constricted. My stomach churned. The nervous system of a child under threat did not understand play; it only recognised danger. Even while running drills, my heart pounded not from exertion but from anxiety and the anticipation of failure.

Representative trials in Brisbane for a Queensland carnival were always a highlight for me, crowded with hundreds of girls, families shouting and cheering. I should have felt belonging. Pride. Strength. Instead, my body stiffened as soon as I stepped on the field. The same dialogue my father spat at me at home-worthless, hopeless, not good enough – played on a loop in my head.

In the first game of the Darling Downs tour, I stood in the outfield. Half an hour in, a ball sailed high over my head. Then another. And another. I ran, but my legs felt heavy, unresponsive. My arms, once springs of strength, trembled as I threw. Each failure created a building sense of panic, tightness in my chest, nausea, and a headache. Hope drained away, replaced by a wave of self-doubt.

Coach called my name. Benched. Replaced.

I stopped. Froze. His words echoed in my body: useless-hopeless-dirty-rotten-mongrel-bastard. I felt each word as a weight pressing into my chest. My shoulders slumped. Hands trembled. Heart racing, I wanted to disappear and vanish into the ground.

Watching from the sideline, powerless, I knew it. I was useless. Every muscle wanted to run, to catch, to throw. Yet my body obeyed the judgement of my mind: shame, humiliation, and the internalised abuse pressed down like a heavy blanket I could not lift.

Regular Saturday mornings of local softball games suddenly brought new humiliation. Dressed in my softball uniform, my mother drove us to a hotel at the Gabba. There, we met Bertie the Bee and Sam the Fizz. I waited anxiously for the green station wagon horn of the Bolton family to arrive to take me to softball.

Inside the hotel sports bar, the clinking glasses, chatter, and stale beer carpet smells swirled around me. I felt utterly invisible. My mother sat with Sam the Fizz, drinking and talking.

Shame pressed down on my chest. Nausea twisted my stomach. My hands fidgeted; my legs bounced under the table. I tried to make myself smaller, hoping no one would notice me; hoping the embarrassment would pass. No family member was interested enough in me to take me to sports, watch me, or acknowledge that I existed outside the chaos of our home.

Mother did not move to wave me off or thank the Boltons for giving up their time and energy to get me to my sport. The Bolton family smiled warmly, laughed kindly, and made space for me in their crowded car. I felt safe with them, but the shame of not being important enough for my own family to do the same clung to me.

As we drove to the field, humiliation remained in my muscles, stomach, and chest. My body tensed, but I held onto hope that on the softball field, with my team, I could finally be seen. At least there, I might matter.

Over the next few games, my body slowly found the inspiration to play the game I loved. Muscles remembered their strength. Legs obeyed. Arms delivered. But my nervous system stayed hyper-vigilant, waiting for the next judgment or echo of abuse. Even victories were tinged with anxiety. Moments of joy would spark, only to be shadowed by tension. The physical cost of mental abuse remained: a body trained for play yet crippled by the constant anticipation of criticism and failure.

Years later, I learned the truth: I was strong and could throw a ball. My body could perform. My mind had been sabotaged by trauma. Realising this was both liberating and deeply sad, a complex mix of vindication and loss. The mental abuse at home had etched itself into every muscle, every breath, every movement.

To outsiders, my parents passed for a perfect couple, impeccably dressed, respected within their political party, and admired for their energy and generosity. My mother, especially, tall, slim, and striking, with smiling eyes that lit up every room, was treated like a woman to be envied. People publicly praised my parents' elegance and polish.

The illusion was convincing.

Communities helped construct that illusion. On Sundays, as we drove to football games to watch my father's favourite team, we passed the local church. My father never allowed us inside. He was fiercely irreligious. I watched families spill out onto the church grounds. The church itself, grand and towering, was a place for very important people. Mothers wore hats and gloves, their

children in party dresses or long pants and ties, and
the fathers in suits; all together in neat, smiling units. I
watched a family holding hands. I wanted to do that. I
so wanted to go inside the church. In my child's mind, I
believed whatever was in that church made people good.
They knew the secret of togetherness. It looked that way
to me, so it must be.

I craved a different kind of father and a more attentive
mother. I wanted to be a better child, one who avoided
trouble.

I wondered whether people on the church grounds had
to line up, as we did at school, to receive the things that
brought them together. Things like feeling important
in their family and being part of a family that had
everything the church provided. Was this thing inside the
church walls? Maybe, I thought, it made them tender,
loving, whole. I imagined they learned it from a teacher,
a minister, someone who knew the secret. Maybe, if I
could be inside, I could understand it and perhaps even
get some for myself. For my family! The guilt for wanting
more was fierce and swirled rapidly. "You deserve
nothing, and that is exactly what you'll get," echoed my
father's words; the self-loathing for wanting more lived
inside me for decades.

The beauty and naiveté of a child's mind are ruthless. I
believed a place could make people calm, whole, and safe.
The secret of togetherness became an obsession, a longing
that grew every week as we drove past, and I could not
enter. I watched the elegance and harmony that came
effortlessly to everyone else.

At home, the illusion was different. Polished clothes and
friendly smiles cloaked tension, but those who got close
eventually saw the cracks. Whispers never matched the
shining surface.

Collusion and illusion: what a confusion I soon learned.

Neighbours who suspected, friends who admired appearances, the community itself – all preferred the comfort of illusion to the discomfort of truth.

In daily life, I learned the code. Appearances meant everything: be tidy, be polite, don't incite trouble. I longed for the togetherness I saw everywhere I looked, though I never truly grasped it. Sometimes I thought it was dispensed like the Bex tablet my mother took for relief, a secret that, once acquired, would guarantee safety and wholeness.

Even then, as a young daughter, I knew what my parents did to me was deeply flawed. It wasn't right for my mother to be punished that way either, especially compared with what I saw on the church grounds or at my cousin's place. No one raised a hand, and definitely no one I saw ever belted their kid or wife, leaving marks on their bodies.

I heard the distant echo of society's recognition that children should be protected, even when the people responsible didn't always understand.

But inside our home, the illusion fell apart completely. Behind the tailored clothes and political speeches, behind the charming smiles and neighbourly conversations, there was fear. Abuse. A child silenced. The illusion gave my parents power but left me invisible.

And yet, that longing never left me. I kept searching for the secret of togetherness, for the tenderness and calm I thought must exist somewhere inside that tall, broad church and the life that seemed so naturally whole for everyone else. I realised so much of what I viewed in the world was bound up in illusion, collusion, longing, and a constant lesson in what the world saw, what it ignored, and what it wilfully chose not to know.

Even the secrets the adults kept, the whispered affairs with Shirley, or Shirleys, were part of the same illusion. Polished appearances masked the truths behind closed doors.

Unsent Letter

Dear Softball Team Manager and Coach,

I am so sorry for messing up the game today.

I tried really hard to focus.

I will try to do better next time.

Unsent Letter

To Whoever First Decided to Use the Word "Normal" for People

I've been thinking about the word normal.

It comes from the Latin word norma, which means a carpenter's square, a tool used to check whether something is straight, aligned, according to the rule.

A perfectly reasonable idea if you're building a table.

You put the square against the wood.

You check the angle.

Yes, that's straight.

Yes, that's aligned.

Very useful for furniture.

But somewhere along the way, we decided to apply that
same idea to people.

Which makes me wonder.

What exactly is the rule we're measuring ourselves
against?

Who wrote it?

Was it the law?

Was it society?

Was it someone's grandmother?

Because you can't measure something against a rule until
you know what the rule is.

And I've yet to see a rule book for families.

Or workplaces.

Or homes.

There is no universal instruction manual that says:

this is the correct angle for a Tuesday afternoon.

This is the proper alignment for a marriage.

This is the approved measurement for raising children.

Yet we still ask the question: is this normal?

Which seems slightly absurd when you think about it.

Because the word actually makes perfect sense when we use it for things.

The teapot sits in the same place on the kitchen bench.

That's it's normal place to be.

The pot plant lives by the window and gets watered every morning.

That's the same place, the normal place for it.

Your shoes are usually by the doorway.

"Mum, do you know where my shoes are?"

"Yes, they're by the door, that's where you always leave them."

That's another example to exemplify the use of the word normal too.

You meet your friends for cards on a Tuesday.

You sit in the same chair.

You take the same walk.

These small repetitions quietly become the map of daily life.

And in that sense, the use of the word normal simply means where things usually are.

Remarkably, though, people are not teapots.

Not pot plants either.

People are certainly not pieces of timber waiting to be checked with a carpenter's square.

More importantly, children, learning about their world, do not live inside explanations.

They live inside atmospheres.

They live inside what they are told

and what happens every day.

Whatever repeats itself becomes the pattern.

And children quietly assume that pattern is normal.

Children don't compare their lives to other lives.

They compare them to yesterday.

And the day before that.
And the day before that.

Whatever repeats itself becomes the compass.

So, *what we often call normal is simply the pattern
someone has grown up inside.*

Which means there isn't one normal.

There are millions of them.

Every house quietly building its own version.

-15-

The Shirley Plan

The outrage in our house rarely stayed hidden for long, at least not from me. Appearances could fool the world, but not the child who watched, listened, and remembered everything. My father's footsteps in the hallway, the hush of my mother's voice whispering to herself in the darkness of our kitchen, and the fleeting comments laced with acidity were cracks in the illusion I had come to know.

So began what I would later call The Shirley Plan. It was more than a betrayal of marriage vows; it was a web of secrecy, charm, and deception, part of the illusion that shaped our lives. Every quiet meeting, every hidden note, every carefully crafted smile contributed to a plan I would only slowly understand.

Even as a child, I could feel its weight sinking into my bones. I didn't know the whole truth, but I couldn't escape the darkness it brought into our home. The fragile stories I clung to of togetherness, elegance, and safety were shattered, and the broken pieces revealed the part of my father hidden from the rest of the world.

It's no secret that my parents controlled my life. That's what happened to a child in their care. I didn't know then, but the happy-ever-after wasn't coming. My father's degradation of my mother and me grew more shocking.

With a thirteen-year age gap between my parents, they met at work on Brisbane's southside. They both lived whole, complicated lives and, years apart, died at age eighty.

My parents were passionate social justice advocates and embraced the lifestyle of their local political groups. They joined, marched, and protested at Brisbane's political forums, surrounded by hundreds who sang and chanted together. I remember the sound and the sight. I loved the music that was both on and under my skin. My mother worked behind the scenes, doing the gritty work that campaigners never see. The first event I attended with her was in Bulimba. A group gathered to prepare sandwiches for the protesters. I didn't understand their cause, but I loved the singing and marching crowd!

Two hours into my first behind-the-scenes event, I grasped the effort it took to produce hundreds of trays of sandwiches. I watched adults work furiously to feed people on city streets. In the long line, everyone knew their job. As a child new to rallies, I was hooked. People, singing, and food: what was not to love? With my family, I joined rallies and loved every moment. I saw, heard, and felt the energy of people united in belief. Each protest felt like a rock concert, with kids hanging out at the back of the crowd.

I loved seeing the speakers clearly, even as they sweated through their rehearsed speeches. They shared stories and beliefs, then led the crowd in song. Best of all, no one cared what the kids did during rally afternoons, so we had the most fun. Every rally, we climbed onto the roof of the park's one-story building. Below us, we watched people shout their messages to others, pushing closer

to the lectern. From our vantage, we heard everything
without having to shout. We thought we were the smart
ones. I loved those rallies for the chance to hang out with
new kids.

My mother and father were deeply involved in the
political party, attending every event. My mother's beauty
and smile concealed her tortured childhood, and her
femininity drew attention in their circles. To my mother,
being glamorous must have felt like a challenge. She was
scrutinised everywhere, which made me wonder whether
her presence burdened my father. Was paying attention to
her a chore for him? His charm was not his only feature
that drew attention.

It was around this same time, when I was still a kid,
that I learned my father was "affairing" with a woman
named Shirley from his political party. Hearing the word
"affair" didn't mean much to me at first, but over time it
became clear: my father was having an affair with Shirley,
perhaps with other Shirleys as well.

How did I know that? Neither parent was secretive about
this conversation. It was like a news broadcast, mainly
in the kitchen, loud enough for anyone to hear each
whimper or scream with crystal clarity.

Eventually, my mother decided to act against her
husband, Shirley, and every other woman he was having
an affair with. One Thursday night after dinner, as she
poured herself a beer in the semi-darkness, she told me
she was going to stuff up his plans with that bloody
Shirley. I watched the cloud-like froth reach the rim
of her glass. I so wanted to sip it, yet never dared. My
mother seemed almost triumphant with her secret. She
didn't share the details with me, but I saw her mind
whirring with the plan as she sat in the darkness with her
drink. I wanted so badly to ask for a taste of the froth on

her beer, but fear and uncertainty held my tongue. Having a plan felt like a miracle! It would stop my father's affairs and fix everything. I wished with every ounce of hope that this would finally turn him from a furious, unpredictable man into someone gentle and kind. My happiness was desperate and secret, built on impossible hope.

The next afternoon, I played our Danny Kaye LP on the record player, still hoping to hear about my mother's plan. I was happy to hear Danny Kaye's beautiful, tender voice and always sang along. He was a political activist, too, which was why his music was allowed to be played on our record player.

Later that night, long after my Danny Kaye singalong had ended, my mother's well-thought-out plan, formed in her darkness, came to light. It was not the good news I had hoped for. The action plan involved me. My mother told my father that he would be taking me to his nighttime meetings from now on. I guessed this was to ensure he could not do the affairing with that bloody Shirley.

My father didn't seem bothered by the plan, but I was. My father's desperation for affairing with a variety of Shirleys meant he secretly upped his risk-taking behaviour and game of jeopardy! I suspected men had a need to win, or was that just my father?

He somehow got his political-party pimp-mates on board, proposed his risk-taking plot, and, voilà, instant babysitters were scheduled so his secret could be played out once again. How I grew to loathe those nights! Being left with strangers while my father disappeared was lonely and terrifying. I lay rigid and silent on their living room floors, anxiously watching the clock until my father came back to claim me. Each time, I felt more deeply trapped in his web of lies. I never knew the people I was abandoned with; the discomfort settled like a chill in my bones. Staying awake until my father returned became a battle against sleep and fear. Yet when we walked back inside our house, he smiled, unbothered, while I wore the worry of his lies on my face, knowing I was forced to play along.

I knew my mother thought we were both at a political meeting. She believed that because of the conversation between my parents when we got home! Or did she? Every time my mother asked about the meeting, a wave of sick panic churned inside me. My father's obsession with Shirley, and all the Shirleys, meant he lied, and forced me to lie too, tying me tighter into the knot of his betrayal.

How many Shirleys was he affairing with, I wondered on those awful nights I was dropped off alone with people I did not know?

How I hated being their kid sometimes, and those nights were some of those times.

It was always a great relief to get into my own bed at the end of those nights. In my bed, I felt safe. Finally, I was where I was supposed to be. There were no lies to tell my mother when I was in bed, and any affair, whatever the heck it was, was over for the night.

There was, however, something even more strange that happened, mainly on those nights once we were home and the lights were out! I became curious about a pattern of sounds that came from my parents' bedroom, next to mine. The pattern, a series of unexplainable yet chilling sounds, kept me awake, leaving me to wonder what was happening.

Bang. Thump. Argh…

The sounds were a mix of fear, hurt, and exhaustion.
First, my mother's voice, loud with accusations against
my father for coming home late. Then came moans
and groans from both of them, followed by my mother
pleading, "Stop." She would cry out, "You're hurting me."
I was sure I could hear her tearful whimpers. There was
no sound from my father. Then came more thumping, in
rhythm, thump, thump against the wall, then her voice
crying out in despair.

I listened intensely, trying to hear if I needed to go to her,
but I didn't. I hadn't heard his voice yet. All darkness,
no more talking. It was unusual not to hear my father's
bellowing voice when my mother was crying in pain, in
his presence!

There it was again, that mix of unexplainable sounds,
not words but aargh, aargh, aargh, in quick succession! It
sounded like he was lifting something heavy, something
really, really, heavy....

I wondered what exactly was happening in that bedroom.
And was my mother okay? What was happening to my
father? What was he lifting in the bedroom? He sounded
like he was really trying hard to do whatever he was
doing, as if his breath was running out. Was my father
okay? He must be. He was always okay!

My good, beautiful, hard-working mother! Had she
been wounded again, even in her own bed! Trying to
sleep through the sounds of my mother's distress was
something I couldn't do; I couldn't fall asleep thinking
about her in agony. The guilt of not rescuing her, if she
needed rescuing, kept my insides boiling, and I had no
chance of sleep for hours.

Then all went quiet.

Relief for me. What happened on these nights, between my mother and father? Was it something to do with the affairing or the lies? The guilt inside me…!

Unsent Letter

Father,

What does affairing truly mean?

What did your affairing say to your wife?

16

Finding a Word

There were times when my mother could take no more abuse, beatings, or verbal tirades. Her mind and body could absorb no more violence from my father. During those times, she would either tell me to get in the car or carry me from my bed to the car. She would then drive to one of two houses: her friend Eileen's or Sam's.

We spent many nights and days in those two homes.

I remember often going to sleep in my bed, only to wake up in a different one. That became everyday life for us. I don't always remember the move from our house to another in the middle of the night.

The time of day or night of our escape determined whether I attended school the next day or for several days afterwards.

Nighttime escapes were the saddest. Arriving unannounced around dinnertime at either home, we would be served a make-do meal. I secretly loved these meals because there was no force-feeding. Seated at the dinner table, I watched my mother cry. Through her tears, she recounted the many blows and abusive incidents she endured, which drove her to flee my father yet again. Listening to her firm statements in her alcohol-saturated state was so sad. She always bore his mark of abuse: a black eye and a busy, confused mind.

"I'm not going back," she stated, "I've had enough of being bashed. I've had enough of his floggings. I can't handle it anymore."

My mother's deep shame sat inside me like a stone. Her sorrow suffocated me, guilt swelling so fierce it nearly drowned me.

Facing them both felt like being trapped in an emotional storm, constantly tossed between fear and the need to stand firm.

Being his daughter was hard; it was shameful at times, even in desperate situations. I struggled with who I was, someone divided between a stubborn love for my parents and the necessity to protect myself from their turmoil. I felt a more profound shame and humiliation every time we escaped the violence of my father, as if each escape left another mark on my identity.

Going to our supporters' homes was uncomfortable. The people who took us in every time we fled his violence at 1-5-8 always made me feel uneasy. Even though I knew I wasn't the abuser or the reason we were running, entering their safety felt awkward.

My heart ached for my mother. I desperately hoped someone would care for her with absolute loyalty, guiding her towards a flicker of hope, away from him.

There were times I doubted my mother's chosen supporters. I was sure her friend Eileen was loyal, having repeatedly proven herself a reliable friend. She would be there for my mother day or night. I trusted and loved Eileen for her support. Eileen and her family always welcomed us warmly, with meals and beds for as long as needed. My mother and Eileen also shared a love of drinking, spending much time discussing ideas for a better life without my father.

Given the messy history, Eileen and her family eventually became our only haven.

My father was not well-liked by either support family or, in fact, by many people. His outlandish ways and bold manner meant many viewed him as "too much" in social settings.

I'm positive many of my parents' friends, and most of our family, didn't understand the reasons my mother remained married to my father, living a life of hell with an unpredictable abuser.

It wasn't a secret that this kind of talk happened. Hearing similar conversations at my parents' friends' political parties always hurt me deeply. The name-calling and insinuations of affairs embarrassed me. Even though I acknowledged it was mostly true, it still felt embarrassing and painful to hear people joke about my father. Penny the Prickle and her friend also told stories in public, saying terrible things about my father, his hostilities, and indiscretions. Hearing that was crushing; I felt ashamed to be his daughter and wanted to protect him from gossip as well.

Hearing stories told quietly, but not quietly enough, always created an argument between my parents. These arguments played out in public, bold, loud, and chaotic, though not as bad as when they happened inside 1-5-8. My father used abusive language and laid angry hands upon her, pushing and niggling her. No one ever stopped him or helped my mother. No one that I can remember.

Witnessing their fights, I wanted to vanish, humiliated; shrinking away, I would snatch what I could grab and flee the party, head down, another night of shame, another scar.

Those nights instilled fear in me; I grew terrified of family outings, always convinced we were unwanted, a burden no one wanted to bear.

I had little faith in that woman, Penny the Prickle, who told stories at the parties. My mother, for some reason, sometimes leaned on that woman for support. Crying on her shoulder, she spilled out much of her life with my father and how hellish it was.

That same woman took me aside one day when we were visiting to tell me, "Your stupid bloody mother doesn't have a clue what's going on in her life."

Her words were like poison. This was the woman who, at times, held my mother in her arms, helping her through her inner ache, showing kindness and compassion.

Her compassion was hollow, cruelly empty. My hatred for her burned. She once told me my mother, broken by infidelity, was herself unfaithful, a betrayal layered on betrayal.

I made sure I had less and less to do with this woman as I learned that, as she held my mother, crying for her husband's infidelities, his abuse, this woman was quite possibly one of the women, one of the so-called Shirleys, sleeping with my father behind my mother's back!

Sickening! That's the word. Mad! Was that the word? Outrageous? I tried to find a word to describe Penny the Prickle, who would undermine a friend, a grieving woman!

I didn't have any words to describe that woman or my father and their affair if it took place.

Those revelations shook my trust in adults. Learning that those I relied on could be deceitful cast a shadow over my ability to confide in others. The very adults who were supposed to offer safety and guidance were more distant and unreliable than ever. From that point on, believing in the sincerity of those around me felt like a gamble I wasn't sure I could afford.

Turning up at Eileen's or sometimes "that woman's" place became something we did at different times and intervals. We left and returned to 1-5-8 for five years, a period I vividly remember. It felt like we were stuck in a washing machine's rinse-and-repeat cycle, except this was live, leave, return, repeat. Just add bruises and broken hearts.

I came to understand that considering my worth was meaningless given my family situation. I knew I was worth nothing to my father and little to my mother. Still, I always ended up rescuing and supporting my mother, consoling her through her darkness and sadness after another flogging. I loved her, worried about her, and felt confused by her. I needed comfort too, which filled me with deep guilt, but it was true. I needed to be part of the care and support.

We learned to accept the chaos of the cycle, wondering what the following day would bring. I tried to take good care of my mother to stop her tears and deep inner ache.

Each time we left our father, I felt guilty about missing the next day of school, and the day after that, and possibly the day after that, depending on how long we were away. My education was derailed by our "family situation", with little hope of catching up on the extended time lost. This disruption in my schooling persisted for years, affecting my ability to engage fully in school and my academic confidence. The gaps in my learning shadowed me, making it difficult to ever truly to catch up, and I often felt out of place among my peers. As an adult, those lost moments in my education have continued to ripple through my life, affecting my career choices and the paths available to me.

Back and forth we went, from one house to another, to escape my father's violence: 10pm, 1am, 4pm. Whenever his unpredictable rage escalated, my mother would grab me and run for safety. Over the years, it became routine. We survived however we could, but I became dead inside, numb to life as I knew it.

News filtered through to us that my father was in hospital on many occasions after we had escaped from him yet again. No visits in the beginning except for my mother. When she returned from a hospital visit, I was keen to hear everything about my father and why he was in the hospital. It was almost always due to a bleeding ulcer. I cried for him and his being ill enough for hospitalisation.

On the one occasion I visited him, I was frightened to see him in his hospital bed, looking pale and sickly. I felt sentimental when I first arrived. When his tears began to fall, so did mine. I felt a pang of sadness when he held out his hand to my mother, and she hesitated before reaching for his. After we left the hospital, I cried again. I felt sick for hours, dull and downhearted, genuinely sad for my father. My mother decided we would return home to look after my father, but she didn't seem very happy about it. I think she looked scared, but she chose to go back to 1-5-8, so we did.

A few days later, home from school, I saw my father, alive, healthy, hammer in hand. Relief and happiness warred with fear and confusion inside me, the sound of his hammer mixing comfort with the chaos I could never escape.

Unsent Letter

Dear Father and Mother

I love the banging sound of

Father's hammer.

It makes me happy.

Makes me feel safe.

-17-
The Returning

Chaos and calamity! Everything that felt remotely like either was yet to change. Abuse continued, we left my father, I missed days of school, and experienced feelings of confusion, many tears; we returned to my father, anxious, agonised, crying hard, confused, numb and daydreaming of a life in peace.

I'm sure my mother and I wished for the same things in life. We spent many nights and days at either Eileen's, Cookie Jackson's, or Prickly Penny's home. I remember going to sleep in my bed, only to wake up in a different one.

I don't always remember the move from our house to another in the middle of the night.

It's 5.30pm, our first night back at 1-5-8 after father's latest hospitalisation. It's a "normal" first night back. We sat at the dinner table, and my parents talk to each other, which was also normal on the first night back.

I went to school the next day, glad to be back to our semi-normal life. I was in my familiar! My bedroom, my bed and pillow, my bathroom, my loungeroom, my clothes, my school uniforms, and my shoes. It always felt good to be back at 1-5-8 after sleeping at other people's houses for a week or more.

Being back at 1-5-8 with all my own stuff felt like reclaiming a piece of normalcy amidst the turbulence.

Two afternoons on with lots of the usual and normal and familiar feely stuff still making me smile, I was beginning to feel kind of okay at 1-5-8.

Just home from softball training, I ran inside, dropped my bags in the laundry, and then headed into the bathroom to shower off the summer heat and training sweat before dinner.

"Mum, I'm starving, what's for din….?"

My mother sat alone in the dark kitchen. Zsstt…

The air felt spooky. My mother stared into space, whispering to herself. I hated this part of her. It wasn't really her I hated, but what had happened to her, what had made her whisper like this. A mix of fear and sadness churned in my stomach, twisting up to my throat. Panic danced on the edges of my consciousness as I wondered if there was anything I could do to help, to comfort her. It was confusing to see her like this, knowing we might plunge back into the chaos we had just escaped. My anger simmered beneath the surface, too, anger at the situation, at my helplessness, at the unfairness that made my life so fragile. I held a storm inside me, each feeling taking turns swallowing the other, leaving me standing there in the dark, grappling with emotions far bigger than myself.

Two days, only two days back! And already…?

No bloody marvellous dinner tonight for my father!

Just my mother, alone in the dark kitchen with her comforter, the anaesthetic of her mental pain, gold and white frothy beer.

I heard my father in his bedroom, noisy in the cupboards!

"Mum?" Leaning against her chair, I looked down to see…what? If she wanted comfort? I didn't know, but I stayed there. I didn't know how to comfort; my mother didn't know how to comfort. I tried anyway.

He appeared in the kitchen doorway and flicked the light switch, making demands as he walked past my mother to the oven.

"And what's for dinner?" he asked smugly, "I've got a meeting at 6.30, and I won't be late!"

"What else is there? Did you make that bread-and-butter pudding?" He opened the oven door, the cold oven, pretending to look for his dinner! Acting!

He looked at his wife! She reluctantly nodded her head.

"Good, I'll have some of that, and custard if there is any left over from last night?" It's sort of, but not quite, a question. It was more of an expectation, an entitlement to have the thing that he wanted at that time.

Oh, please, please, Mum, my mind willed, there must be some of last night's custard left! I hoped like crazy there was some in the fridge!

My father turned towards the kitchen table where my mother was seated.

"Oh, on the grog, are you? Again! Can't stop the
grog, can ya, just like the rest of your family. Drunks!
Imbeciles! Mongrel-bastards!"

My mother did not raise her eyes, not once.

The thunderous man was back. Same fuel, same demons,
same vessel….

And…she was back, sadly, believing his promise to
change.

Same…same…same….

And me too, I was back as the same kid.

My hand softened on her shoulder as I sat to comfort and
protect her. My mother was too "everything" to fight my
father that night: too sad, tired, worn out, lost, too….

I bowed lower to look at her face. My eyes met hers, both
filled with tears. Her grief moved inside me. Hell! I saw
a bruise, an angry purple mark on her cheekbone, left by
my father's hand. A cold realisation settled in my chest,
reminding me of what he was capable of. Her slumped
body, the bow of her head, her stillness was different
when she was still because of him.

Her silence and the dinner he was looking for wasn't
cooked because of him. He could have bread-and-butter
pudding and last night's custard for dinner. I suspected
she made that at morning tea-time before her midday
nap.

A loud knock on the door startled me, but it didn't
raise my mother's gaze; it sure raised my father's. Still
searching the fridge for the custard, he looked up to see
Bertie the Bee, my least favourite man, standing at the

top of the steps, holding a large, wet brown paper bag. I would bet he had his usuals inside: six tallies, cold, wet bottles of beer!

Bertie stumbled into the kitchen and dropped skewwhiff onto the same seat he always did at the top of the table; my father's seat!

He plonked the brown paper bag onto the table and said, "Hey kiddo, grab an opener, will ya?"

Bertie the Bee was already walking and talking the language of sixteen beers in his belly, seated on his "big fat arse" as he called it. My breath drew itself deeply inside me. I knew before I knew that this was going to be really something.

The anxiousness in my gut made me nauseous straight away. I always felt that way when Bertie the Bee visited, especially when the visit was a surprise, like this one!

The tallies rattled as Bertie the Bee put them in the door of our refrigerator. Grabbing a glass without invitation, he poured himself and my mother another beer. He glugged the first glass of liquid gold straight down his throat. He sighed, licking his lips and pouring his next, all the while eyeballing my father. He asked my father what he'd been up to lately. The response came quickly, "Working."

Bertie the Bee kept asking the same question, and my father kept repeating his answer. The tension was growing, and the pace at which beers were downed was increasing. My mother yelled at him to stop acting like an idiot.

"You live with an idiot. You must be okay with having idiots around!"

My hand shot to my mother's leg in panic. I held on
tightly as she looked past me towards the front door,
drawing on her cigarette. Sitting this close to two
intimidating grown men was overwhelming. I wanted to
run to the safety of my bedroom, but I knew better than
to run from Bertie the Bee. He would follow me, and I
didn't like that. I would be made to explain why I ran
away, and I didn't like that either.

Bertie the Bee saw my mother's red cheek. Oh no. I knew
what that meant. Threats to kill my father if he hit his
wife again and vile name-calling followed.

Bertie the Bee got out of his seat, moving towards my
father, who stepped quickly out of the way.

"Get back here, you wife basher," Bertie the Bee called.
"A man doesn't hit a woman. You're not a man. You're
a flea. You touch a woman, any woman, again, Len, you
mongrel, and I'll get all my mates, and we'll give you the
biggest hiding you've ever had, right? You hear me?"

My father, standing just out of reach, did not look too
bothered. My mother and I were.

"Stop it. Stop arguing," she cried out in panic. "You've
had too much to drink."

Knock, knock. "Ya there, love? It's Sam, Sam the Fizz.
Come to see how ya goin'?"

No way! Sam the Fizz! It couldn't be! I didn't think I
could breathe.

Aside from Bertie the Bee visiting, the next worst
thing that could happen was Sam the Fizz visiting at
the same time as Bertie the Bee! It was truly the most
uptight, breathless, and hypervigilant I had ever been,

because I knew I would witness violence. It was all those exhausting, scary things, as well as hugely chaotic and perilously dangerous to everyone in the house and nearby.

When the two men visited together, when both had drunk a little, it was sort of okay and not as scary. But when they had both had like six bottles each, the police were usually called.

The most worrying part of Bertie and Sam's visits was that they had the same temperament as my father. All had explosive tempers and killer attitudes; all were physically strong, with short fuses, and loved bloody, explosive fist fights.

The difference between Bertie, Sam, and my father, however, was that they protected my mother from her cruel husband when they decided it was time to teach him a lesson. The animosity between the two sides began long before I was born and continued throughout my life, with all its threats, abusive insults, torment, and fistfights.

Bertie the Bee threw his tattooed arm forward, his rounded fist landing on my father's forehead and knocking him into the kitchen sideboard. My father looked stunned. I was shaken. My mother screamed! My father, dazed, had eyes of dread, while Bertie, my mother's protector, squared up like a boxer, moving on his feet. Another punch was imminent. My father moved. The swing missed! The boxer stumbled, and my father roared, "Drunks, you're all the same. Dirty-rotten-mongrel-bastard-good-for-nothings can't even stand to fight. You, germ."

"You prick. You bastard," shouted Sam the Fizz as he ran in, swinging at my father. "I'll knock you out, you mongrel. I know you flogged your wife. You're gonna cop a bigger hiding than the one she got, you bastard."

The swinging punch landed, and my father hit the lino floor hard. My mother screamed at the rage playing out in her kitchen. She was overawed. My father yelled out in fright, cowering, his arms over his face, "Stop, stop!"

He was floored, trapped by the two protectors, there to take revenge on him, right then, in that moment. They both kicked at my father, yelling words I didn't understand. I took off, fast, running out the back door, down the stairs, and hiding under the house. I knew my mother was safe. I couldn't watch any more of the fighting in my kitchen. It sounded so loud when sweaty, angry fists of skin hit skin, and I was right there, close to the fighting. I wanted them both to stop hurting my father. He was so scared, and I couldn't watch his terrified face. It made me feel sorry for him.

I jumped a couple of fences and ran up the neighbour's stairs, calling out, "Mr Howard, call the police. Please call the police."

I heard voices near our back steps as I lay flat on the neighbour's steps. My heart felt like it was going to burst. Leaping out of our back door, my father raced around the side of the house, followed by Sam the Fizz and then Bertie the Bee. I heard my father shouting, crying out for help, and the sounds of panic. The chasers were promising him death. The scary sound of my father's frightened pleading voice faded into the distance.

Running down the neighbour's steps, I jumped the fence and ran back into our house.

I cried. Cried the same tears I cried for the same reasons I always cried.

Zsstt.

All was quiet. The house was dark, and my mother sat alone until I sat with her.

The police arrived. No sirens, just the darkness in our house. My mother spoke with them for a short time, then they left.

I didn't see my father again that night, nor did I see Bertie or Sam either, thank goodness! Fear had left the theatre of 1-5-8 for the evening.

I sat beside my mother and looked at her.

She stared at the wall.

I loved her! I felt such sadness for her. How could I help her?

She continued to stare at the wall.

"You're weak," she said.

I said nothing. I couldn't!

"You're weak. You cried for him in the hospital. You're the reason he bashes me; I get bashed for leaving him. Then I come back because of you and your tears, and get bashed again. You're weak. You'll-be-taken-advantage-of-your-whole-life. Toughen-up-girl. Stop-being-so-weak. Stop-getting-me-b-a-s-h-e-d."

I sat there, her words cutting through the air and embedding in my mind. Hearing her say I was the cause of her bashing made my heart sink under the weight of guilt and confusion. Her words echoed in my head for years, replaying during quiet moments, each time leaving a deeper scar. It made me question my worth and whether love would always come with pain.

Even now, I sometimes wonder how much of that night was truly my fault, and how those scars shaped who I became.

I cried; cried for my father being beaten by the two friends, who beat my father for beating my mother; and I cried for myself, beaten by my father, who beat my mother for leaving him.

I

lived

numb.

But in that numbness, I began to consider my next steps. Each tear, each accusation, pushed me to seek understanding amid the chaos. I sensed that change was needed and that a future beyond this turmoil was possible. Contemplating what might come next offered a faint glimmer of hope, even as I struggled to process the night's events.

Unsent Letter

Dear Bertie and Sam,

What the hell? Are you being helpful?

Or not? I still can't work it out!

Unsent Letter

Dearest Mean-Spirited Mother

Please share with me how exactly I made my father

hit you, this time?

Unsent Letter

Dearest Meanest Father,

I felt sad when Bertie and Sam hurt you.

It hurts my insides to see you so scared.

This is very confusing to understand inside my brain,

but Father, I do care

about you. Sometimes!

-18-

Untethered

Winning our netball game was fantastic, and the day got even better when Jennifer offered me a lift home in her brother's car. It was cold and windy, so I was thankful not to be out in the weather for the next few hours. I excitedly and gratefully jumped into the backseat of the little cream V-dub and drove from one side of Brisbane to the other.

The V-dub was noisy and rattled like crazy, but it was better than catching two buses and a train, then walking home in the dark.

It was about 5.30pm when the sun vanished from my world for the day. I loved that time of day. Paul, Jennifer's brother, pulled his noisy V-dub into the curb outside my house.

"Thank you so much," I called back, running into our driveway and around to the back door, our usual entry place.

I smiled, though it was freezing, as I rushed up the back stairs and through the doorway. To my surprise, both my parents stood just inside. A welcoming party?

No! Immediately, I noticed my mother was tense, and my father was infuriated.

The tension thickened, and the air hit me the moment I entered, so I froze, not daring to move another step.

No smiles or happiness greeted me, only that look. My father's face showed there was a serious problem. He ordered my mother, "Grab the belt."

I scarched his face for any clue. His expression shifted to deep red, jaw tight, teeth clenched. He ran his tongue along his bottom lip, breathing heavily.

My body grew rigid, still. My mother returned with the leather belt, an awkward half smile on her face, reminding me of a Labrador pup retrieving a ball: just a game, a playful game.

It was pathetic to witness. And frightening.

Suddenly, he stepped forward and grabbed my neck with both hands, digging his fingers in, shaking me back and forth, yelling, "You slut, you dirty rotten little slut, where have you been? You've been in a sex wagon, haven't you?"

He hurled me across the floor. I landed hard against the back wall.

"You slut."

He spat the words, grabbed the belt from my mother, and glared at me. I stood shakily, watching him wrap the belt around his hand in slow motion.

I began to speak in a gentle, delicate, pleading voice, a tone that would not make my father angrier. My breath was shortening in panic, and I felt the tears coming.

"Dad, you know him. He is your friend Bobby's son, Paul, Jennifer's brother. He drove Jennifer and me home from netball."

There was no response. I could see in my father's eyes that he'd left the conversation. He'd already gone into his head, into inner storm mode. He was somewhere in a full wind squall, smashing houses and everything in its path.

I was one hundred and fifty percent correct.

My father flicked the belt at me like a whip. His weapon.

The next fifteen minutes were a storm of his violence, his arm thrashing the belt into my body, enacting the punishment he always threatened.

His breathless words, syllables, and the belt struck me in unison: "You-will-not-ride-in-sex-wag-ons-ag-ain-you-dir-ty-rot-ten-mon-grel-of-a-sl-ut. You-will-not-ride-ho-me-from-spor-t-in-sex-wag-ons-ag-ain-you-dir-ty-rot-ten-mon-grel-sl-u-t."

He gripped my arm, whipping strike after strike with his favourite belt, degrading me with his words.

I bent to hold my arms over my legs to stop the belt from hitting them, eventually slumping onto the floor once again.

The stinging was deep, but humiliation and shame cut deeper. Outrage rose, only to be crushed by his rage. I noticed blood seeping from cuts I hadn't seen before and welts forming.

I saw blood on the floor. Would I be beaten for that, too? Should I move or stay? Panic rose as I spotted blood on my white socks.

I tried to crawl away, but slipped, probably on my sweat or blood. I can't remember where the last strike landed.

Leaving my body, I floated upwards, watching the thirteen-year-old girl shield her face and legs with her arms, waiting out the storm. Watched as the madman slashed my skin. It was sad, seeing her and me brutalised from this distance.

Was this the safety I provided for myself, to disassociate?

My eyes could no longer see. I could not register my father's presence, nor was I conscious of the bystander, my mother. I blinked and blinked. I tried to get up.

When I could finally see again, I was alone. After every beating, I was alone. I noticed a heaviness in my chest, stinging in my legs, and shame swelling in my stomach. Worthlessness and hopelessness spun in my head, losing in a lopsided fight.

Blank again. Nothing worked in my head. I slowly edged towards what I hoped was the bathroom; pain faded into numbness. I was unsure which way to go, but I just wanted to reach the safety of the bathroom and close the door.

Hurting all over, I pushed the door shut and collapsed on the cold tile floor, gasping for breath as tears fell.

I inched my netball uniform off my skin, bit by bit, depending on what hurt the most and if I could reach all the bits to pull them off. Lying on the bathroom floor felt okay, better than out there where I was. I couldn't see the blood on the Lino floor from inside the bathroom.

No, I screamed inside. I saw blood on my school netball skirt too.

Standing under the trickling, lukewarm water, I kept adjusting the water pressure to minimise the sting on my wounds. The bruising was starting to show, with more welts rising on my thighs and lower legs. There were a couple on my arms as well, so I leaned further under the shower stream to ease the sting on my tender skin.

I stood under the shower for a long time, exhausted all over! I stood with sadness in my bones, wondering why he had hit me. Why did he hit me like a madman? Why was I the target of another senseless flogging?

The answer to this question remained unknown for many decades.

I felt myself grieving for another girl, not me, but someone else enduring this pain. Even as I saw the marks and felt the hurt, it was almost as if I was outside myself, disconnected from reality. Numbness settled over me, too heavy for tears or questions. My mind was overwhelmed by exhaustion and humiliation.

I found two of the softest, darkest towels in the bathroom linen cupboard and patted my skin dry with one. I tried not to get any blood on the towel, even though it was dark. I crossed my fingers that the blood wouldn't show. I took ages to dry myself. Grabbing the second towel, I tiptoed the confused, sad, aching girl to her bedroom and put on very little, so very little material touched the sore, swollen, broken skin. I placed the dry towel on the bedsheets to catch the blood that would fall during the night. It felt incredibly uncomfortable to lie on sore, swollen legs and arms. It was hard to soothe my drained, bleeding body and shattered mind.

From my warm bed, yet with discomfort all around, my over-tired mind kept asking why? Why did my mother stand by and watch my father thrash me, her kid, again? Why? Why didn't they drive me to the netball game, or at least pick me up to make the trip easier? And when did it become a crime to be driven home by a friend's brother? More importantly, why was I labelled a slut?

Four decades of wisdom have cocooned a little of the heartache as I try to find answers to my whys. I continue to wonder, though, why they treated me so?

Unsent Letter

Dear Father, who I don't want to be my father,

I know you lost control today in the bashing frenzy.

Is this kind of frenzy going to become usual?

I want to tell the police, because I know you aren't

supposed to hit me like that.

From your petrified daughter.

Unsent Letter

Dear Petrified Mother of Mine

Why did you stand frozen while watching me,

your daughter, being victimised,

my body violated by my father,

who had ten times the strength of me!

Too petrified to speak up? Are you?

Fear of being his next victim?

I am so confused!

Your confused, battered daughter.

-19-
As Witness

To the two of you,

I wanted to write you a letter,
So, I did.
But…I never sent it.

I kept thinking you might stop blaming each other.
Or that someone would make you stop.
I kept hoping your marriage wasn't as bad as it seemed.
As it looked to me.

I watched you try to hold things together,
Like something that had cracked,
That kept slipping.
Is that why you didn't reach out to
Protect me?

You said it was fine.
But it didn't look fine.
I hoped I was wrong.

I wondered if you had ever been in love.
I really did.
Because I didn't understand how love
could sound like that.
I knew people were allowed
to fall out of love.
What I didn't understand

122

Was how someone could be hurt
yet it did not count
Unless someone wrote it down.

I thought marriage was meant to fix things.
Everyone said it does.
The dresses.
The suits.
The promises.
But nothing seemed to change.

I kept waiting for you both to be happy.
Or for someone to say that
It wasn't working.
No one did.
So, I watched.
And I remembered.

-20-
Love...Bites

I was woken the next morning around 4am for the follow-up game once again. The Tiger's Milk shoved in my face as I looked up to see the fake smile of my live-in assassin!

I drank the drink, loathed the bloke, packed the bags, and slid into the car next to him! He's driving me to the pool. Urgh and yay!

I really didn't want to swim! My body, with its raised bumps, broken, raw skin, and bruising, was ignored by him as usual, yet I was unable to ignore the wounds this time. My legs were hideously tender, sore, and uncomfortable, my neck aching, and my mind filled with resentment, but I went!

As the car rounded the sharp corner towards the swimming pool entrance, the passenger-side door next to me swung open, and I followed, rolling out onto the road. My legs stung as my battered body hit the bitumen. My knees and shoulders hurt, and my hands were grazed, beginning to bleed. The monster continued driving towards the swimming pool. It was not unusual for the passenger door to randomly swing open!

Maybe the person entering the passenger seat is to blame. Are they concerned! Scared to join the driver, so don't close the door quite properly as an oversight?

Refer to Family DNA, Section "History of bad ideas", for an almost decent, believable response.

I drank the disgusting drink. I smiled the "thank you for offering to drive me to swimming training" smile, and that was all he was getting from me. How was I going to survive being his daughter for the rest of my life? Seriously, how? I knew I could not endure his abuse, AND hide the physical marks, AND hide the emotional burden while living this life. I went to school, played sports, saw my friends, and went to parties. It was impossible.

Too much tiger's milk, too much pressure to pretend, too much of my father was happening to even consider trying to regulate any part of my body! Dropping my heavy school bag onto the grass, I held the towel wrapped around my body, right until the moment I slid into the shallow end of the pool. The water felt icy cold, yet the other kids in the swimming squad appeared to be loving it. I felt so uncomfortable that I was unsure if I could swim; walking itself was a struggle that morning.

The welts and cuts on my legs and arms felt the icy water more than any other part of my body. They all stung, all felt giant-sized as the water enveloped me, but I didn't look down at any of them.

When the second hand hit the thirty on the large clock, the coach called "go," and I went, swimming freestyle, up the left-hand side of the lane, then back down the right. I was swimming slowly because it was all I could manage, but it felt good as I warmed up. It was always my favourite part of the training: the warm-up. I could think more clearly in the slow-motion state of flow, where I forced my arms out as far as possible and let my legs kick freely. I didn't always do a tumble turn because it made me dizzy, leaving me disoriented for a while, which reminded me of the dizziness I felt lying on the linoleum floor at home. I didn't do a tumble turn because my legs wouldn't bend easily, and it hurt too much.

Whistles, shouts, splashes, and laughter in the swimming training environment always made me freer. This was my place, where I felt free with my friends, and I loved swimming. The hour and a half flew by, and I grabbed my towel as quickly as I could, wrapped myself, and made my way to the change rooms. At the end of each swimming session, I usually felt exhausted for a brief time, then sparked up once again. Today I did not.

No one said anything to me about the marks on my body, so I escaped having to explain, especially so early in the morning. I wasn't yet sure what I would say if asked. I showered carefully, then gently patted my cold, sore legs and arms. Dressing in my school uniform took a bit longer than usual. Brushing my hair into two pigtails, I packed my swimming bag into my school bag and began the walk to the bus stop.

The short-sleeved, collared shirt hid my upper body marks from the previous night's thrashing, but my arms and legs would be on show at school. I'd have to make up a story and be that person, the one who pretended everything in her life was okay when asked about the marks on my body. Nothing new! Another lie, another manipulation, more guilt!

I walked the short distance to the bus stop, then began the double bus journey to school.

The smell of chlorine usually stayed in my hair all day at school, and I loved it because I felt like I had done something special for myself, something that made me a stronger and better person.

There was very little room in the bag racks, so I shoved my school bag, filled with the chlorine-soaked swimming bag, in somehow and went inside the classroom. I sat in the same seat each morning: middle row, middle seat. Chatty students filled the room as my morning form class began.

All went quiet as our home room teacher arrived.

I heard my name called and looked to the teacher.

"Yes?"

"Come out the front, please!"

I pointed to my chest, "Me?"

"Yes," said the teacher!

I'm rarely surprised to hear my name called for no reason. I became used to it at my house. Yet this morning I was.

"Will you come up the front and stand here, please! That's right, come up, stand at the front," she said again!

"Now, please turn around and face the class. Thank you, that's it. Stand still."

"Class," said the teacher in a loud voice, "Don't be silly. Sit still. This young lady will be standing in front of the class for a while. I'll get back to you all in a moment."

I wondered what I was doing standing in front of my classmates, why they were looking at me, and why I was looking at them. I didn't understand why I was standing at the front of the class that morning.

I couldn't see behind me, but I thought the teacher had left the room because I heard her shoes walking out of the door onto the wooden veranda. Next, I listened to what sounded like people walking towards our classroom, and the footsteps on that same veranda grew louder and louder.

Still sitting still, my classmates started to pull weird faces, and we all laughed a little.

The deputy principal and the teacher arrived together, spoke sternly to the class, telling them to be quiet because they had something essential to do. The class went silent and stayed that way. I knew that the deputy principal's presence in the classroom was serious. He could hand out detentions if anyone misbehaved, so I took it seriously, too.

The teacher walked towards me, then the deputy principal. I notice that my school buddy, a year eleven female student, also arrived. My buddy stood close to me at the front of the class as well.

Something strange was about to happen; I sensed it. I noticed the teacher and the deputy principal were holding wooden rulers. I started to worry, scared about what they would do with the rulers. I was still standing in front of the class, looking at them as they looked back at me, and I suspected they were also watching the wooden rulers in the two adults' hands.

The adults then moved the rulers towards the hem of my school uniform and began lifting it. I looked down, thinking my school uniform must not be the right length, still confused about why I was undergoing this unusual experience.

Then it fell into place. I raised my head to see the stunned looks on some students' faces as they witnessed the examiners' findings. The two adults slowly examined my legs, revealing the full extent of last night's vicious attack: the welts, the bruises, and the belt slices on my lower and upper legs. Then they realised I had the same affliction on my arms.

I gazed upwards, my mouth closed, breathing in long, slow breaths through my nose. There I stood, shaking, alone, and on display in my shame and humiliation. I stood stiffly in front of the class as the two adults leaned in for a closer look, circling and lifting my uniform from front to back. No words were exchanged. The room was eerily silent as I looked anywhere but at anyone. My school uniform was eventually lowered, and I could breathe a little more easily again.

Back in my usual classroom seat, I stared at the blackboard, not turning my head. I could hear students whispering. I couldn't make out exactly what they were saying, but it was probably about the examination. Nothing more was said to me or about me during that morning's form class. The form class morning messages were read aloud to the class, and we left for the rest of the day's lessons.

Still embarrassed and humiliated, I was overcome with shyness. If I could have been invisible in that classroom, I would have chosen that option and stayed that way for the rest of the school day. I was quiet for most of the day anyway, if not invisible. A teacher and I did, however, have words later that afternoon, which was precisely when I felt my own fire....

I had tried hard to be a normal girl that day, the other girl I had to be when I was out in the world, the girl who did not live in the house at 1-5-8 Lavandar Avenue, or have wounds on her body that people could see. It was hard to be that other pretend-normal girl that whole school day, as some kids pointed out the injuries on my body to kids who didn't know about them. I chose not to explain the story and ignored others' comments for the rest of the school day.

At lunchtime, it was time to change into my sports uniform. This time, I changed in private, alone in a bathroom stall. After carefully removing my school uniform, I put on my sports skirt, which was shorter, then my sports top, which had no sleeves or collar. I knew this would show more of my body, including the bruises and cuts, but what could I do?

I arrived at my next lesson, history, which I always found so interesting, and which took place right before the sports lesson.

The teacher and class were settling in when the teacher looked at me, then did a double-take. Staring curiously at me, she called, in her loud screechy voice, "Stand up, thank you."

Of course, I was unhappy about having to stand up again, but I did it, ever so gradually. I was doing everything ever so gradually that day.

As I slowly pushed my chair from my desk, the teacher called again, louder this time, "Do as you are told. Stand up, little town flirt!"

I was stunned! I replied, "Pardon? What? Little town flirt?"

The seemingly irritated history teacher said, "It doesn't take much to work it out, does it, little town flirt!"

Stumbling for words myself, I called straight back, "What do you mean?"

"What's on your neck?" she spat out!

I didn't understand her words and didn't care for her by that point. I picked up things on my desk, walking hurriedly from her room before I said something I regretted. I was both embarrassed and angry.

I heard her voice calling me to return to my seat as I left the room. I didn't.

I couldn't bear to listen to her for another moment. Did she not see the marks on my body? Did she wonder how they got there? Did she think to ask me? Why did the thing she saw on my sore neck make me a little-town flirt, and what was on my neck, anyway?

-21-

Rulers

I couldn't breathe for the tenth time that day! Grabbing my school bag, I went straight to the girls' toilets. Looking in the mirror, I saw two minor reddish-purple bruises.

One on each side of my neck.

I was in my own simmering fury, no longer simply angry, but ferociously mad at my father! My father had caused me enough problems at school with the marks on my body, but now the marks on my neck, the bruises from where he grabbed me as he threw me to the floor, had made things worse. Memories of his attack flooded my mind again.

I slumped on the wooden bench, trying to think straight as my brain wasn't working correctly. I couldn't think straight. This day was too much for me.

I needed to escape this school, leave the history teacher behind, distance myself from my father, and finally move on with my life. I didn't know if I wanted to go home to scream in my madness at my father or run as far as I could until I couldn't run any further.

I was exhausted from overthinking and trying to figure out the next right thing to do.

My energy wasn't up to telling my father what I wanted to say. My mind was filled with screaming hellfire, just like he yelled at me. I wanted to scream at him about what my day had been like; in fact, about what my body felt like, along with what my day had been like. I wanted to scream at him, "You need to know what you are doing to me."

But I didn't. When I arrived home, I didn't tell my father anything about what had transpired that day. Not one thing. I lacked the courage and energy to cope with the hiding that might have been his response, which would have sealed my fate of yet one more conflict.

I needed to think some more. Standing under the flow of the warm shower, I allowed the water to fall for as long as it took for me to clear my mind. The extra-long shower was perfect, and the jigsaw puzzle fell perfectly into place as he yelled at me for wasting water. I ignored him.

That judgmental teacher, who was skilled in recalling her specialty topics but not in reading people, suspected the bruising on my neck was from love bites.

And those suspected love bites made me a Little Town Flirt?

Was that what she was assuming? Love Bites? Little Town Flirt?

I bet it was, the cow!

Unsent Letter

Dear small-minded, mean teacher,

Your job is to teach me and

look out for my well-being.

You didn't do either today

I'm ringing the police about you, too.

They will help me work out how to

Be in the world with people like you.

Unsent Letter

Dear Me

My mind is at an emotional and mental low.

I think if I lived on a secluded farm,

somewhere rural and quiet,

It would be easier

not because I don't want people,

But because I wouldn't have to present.

I wouldn't have to see anyone

except my family.

I wouldn't have to function at my peak,

or perform in the mainstream,

or pass as normal, capable, fine.

It would give me relief

from having to be

a functional person

when I am not.

-22-
Wind Chimes

Contemplation brought me the image of wind chimes. Not delicate, garden-variety chimes. These were wind chimes in a storm: always moving, never quiet, sometimes banging together, sometimes whispering, sometimes vibrating straight through my chest, sometimes delicate enough to catch sunlight and make me squint.

Trauma felt like those chimes. I could tell myself, stop listening, don't pay attention. But they rang anyway.

They had to.

Because my body remembered.

Because my mind hadn't caught up.

Because they were there.

Sometimes they banged together so loudly.

I laughed at the absurdity.

Sometimes they swung gently and nearly disappeared.

One would clang and knock another, like siblings arguing over nothing, and the sound ricocheted across the room.

A small one would twist in the wind and hum a high little note that seemed almost like a giggle.

Then the sun would hit another just right, and it would glitter so brightly I had to squint, shielding my eyes, as it rang against the others.

The vibration went right through me, as though the metal and the wind had memorised every ache I'd ever carried.

I tried to close my eyes and imagine silence.

To tell myself to stop hearing them.

It didn't work.

They were not wrong, bad or cruel. They simply existed.

And they weren't leaving.

As I watched them, I noticed how one seemed to lean into another as if trying to help. How the smallest one would suddenly swing alone.

I could feel the gentle hum in my chest, and just for a moment, allowed it to be nothing more than sound. Reminding me that I was still here.

That I had survived.

Listening didn't mean I had to fix anything or control them.

I could just let them move through me.

That was enough.

I invite you to pause for a moment, to listen for your own wind chimes. Those little noises or movements in your life that keep ringing, even when you try to ignore them.

Can you notice them without trying to fix them?

Can you let them be just as they are?

Guilt and intimidation overwhelmed me when I tried to consider my needs. My parents instilled guilt deeply. My hurt would leave, then return; it never ended. Journaling later helped my healing begin, as I learned to trust my observations inside 1-5-8.

Healing wasn't about changing my parents; I aimed to be the kind of kid I wanted to be, even knowing they wouldn't change. My gut affirmed this through constant anxiety. My healing had to come from within, by being the best kid I could be to stop the churn inside me.

Living with nausea stole joy from me. Accepting my journey, I realised I could not change my parents, who hurt me deeply, never validating my pain or honesty. Surviving those tumultuous years, I slowly began to re-parent myself, meeting my own emotional needs, like sitting with the nasturtiums or listening to music on the radio. This ongoing process helps me care for myself and, quietly, my adult children and grandchildren.

Healing led me through many destinations as I searched for calm. I often found myself in the wrong places: chanting affirmations, doing yoga, meditation, and solitude, but none worked as I had hoped.

Ultimately, I discovered contemplation as a way to continue my search for inner peace. Unlike the drain of continual overthinking, true contemplation gave me peaceful company, letting me stay with misery without drowning in it.

Contemplation.

Not something I asked for.

It came in the disguise of overthinking.

Loops, circles, endless turning.

I thought it was only noise,

but in the noise, I found pauses.

A shape forming.

A truth surfacing.

Contemplation doesn't solve.

It waits.

It lets the wound breathe.

And sometimes that is enough.

As I sat in contemplation, I noticed it did not erase or remove my trauma, which I wished for desperately. Instead, contemplation stayed with my confusion, offering space to see my hurt clearly without being consumed by it. This taught me that healing doesn't mean forgetting but instead engaging with and understanding pain.

Contemplation stayed beside my body as it trembled, steady and patient, letting me see my deepest wounds without being overwhelmed. I learned to face and process trauma to begin to heal my insides and mind. My mind grew calmer, and the anxious hamster in me rested. I felt peace, which is healing at work. I'm endlessly thankful for contemplation.

Unsent Letter

Dearest Loving Cousins,

I know you have sugar in your Milo

But that's not the reason I want to

live with you.

I realised this in contemplation.

-23-
Astonishments

With a family holiday arranged, I happily packed my holiday clothes into my school bag. Leaving my bedroom for the car, I felt as happy as I could be.

Ahead were peaceful days for us all. I was happy knowing there would be no 6.30 fight nights, blackouts, or floggings. I would eat food prepared by others in a different kitchen. And the kitchen rules would be their rules.

Our car was finally packed full of holiday bags and happy holiday makers, and my father began the long drive to southern New South Wales. This was the first holiday. Then we'd drive back to 1-5-8 only to be off again soon after to our Ari Bay holiday, which included fishing and swimming.

The road trip was thrilling as the endless road unfolded before us, the rumble of semis echoing in the air. At thirteen and a half, I was more curious than ever to see New South Wales come to life beyond the pages of my geography book, a subject I struggled with at school. Reading maps felt like deciphering an impossible code, but after seeing the landscapes firsthand, with rolling hills and vast open skies, everything started to make more sense.

After one long, full day's drive, we finally arrived at our holiday address, ready to spend time out of the car and off the busy highways. My father easily found the address of Bertie the Bee's retired friends. Tim and Molly were providing our accommodation for the next seven days.

We spent most of our time with Tim and Molly exploring the southern New South Wales district, visiting some of its beautiful beaches, and planning to catch the circus in town, which we were really looking forward to.

It was Friday night, and we had two days left. About six o'clock, as dinner was being served, Tim mentioned the roller-skating rink nearby. That's precisely where I spent the next four hours, having the most fun I'd ever had on a holiday. I had a blast rolling around as music blared and coloured lights flashed on and off, one after the other, creating a party atmosphere at the fan-filled skating rink. The rink was full of people having just as much fun as I was. As we rolled around, I heard one of the sun-tanned, long-haired, surfer-looking boys shout to his friends, "Come on, let's see who can stay upright the longest!" Their carefree energy was infectious, and it wasn't long before I was swept up in the laughter and excitement. A short time later, I noticed those same boys at one end of the rink.

They were in hysterical laughter, struggling to balance on their skates, then falling like full-bodied acrobats to the floor again. I could not recall ever seeing anyone laugh so hard, and their constant tumbling made me laugh too. My stomach hurt from the laughter. I stopped at the other end of the rink to catch my breath. Abruptly, the loud music stopped, and an announcement was made to the skating crowd.

"Skaters, please stop skating."

The announcer named the first game of the evening. All skaters needed a partner. One of the surfer boys, who kept falling and getting back up, skated over to me. He held out his hand and asked me to be his partner. He was gorgeous, blonde-haired and blue-eyed, and we skated off together. Each time we passed his mates, who were still laughing, we smiled and laughed with them. I loved it, skating together around the rink. I had the most smiley, fantastic night as we skated together in every game.

The night came to an end, and before we said goodbye, Mark asked if he could see me again. I was astonished. What a surprise to go skating in a town thirteen hours from my house to meet Mark. I felt so happy that I said yes. My family and I were going to the circus the next afternoon, so I invited Mark to come along.

As my family arrived at the circus, I was excited to see Mark waiting outside. We all sat together, laughing at the clowns and animal acts. I enjoyed every moment of the afternoon. I felt like I was in a fairy tale, surrounded by crowds and a gorgeous boy who took an interest in me and treated me like I mattered. In my sweetheart state of mind, Mark and I smiled all afternoon. Secretly, I hoped our affection showed my parents I was more than just a surface-level presence. I hoped they saw I was worth knowing.

With a face that had smiled all afternoon and skin that was goose-bumpy, I wasn't ready for the afternoon to end. We stayed a little longer to chat about the acts, the animals, and the big, colourful circus tent. To my surprise, Mark asked my parents if he could drive me home. It was extraordinary; they said yes. Seated in the front seat of his car, right alongside him, Mark drove me to Tim and Molly's house, just five minutes away. We sat together in his car talking for ages. This was a new experience; I felt so grown-up. Mark talked about surfing, and I talked about my love of sports. Mark was leaving for Sydney the next morning, and I was heading back to Brisbane, then off to Ari Bay.

We talked about friends, our lives in different cities, and much more. It felt bittersweet; time had flown by. Then, we kissed a proper, beautiful, soft goodbye kiss: another surprise, but one I adored. I kissed a grown-up boy, a proper kiss. And it was him, the gorgeous, well-mannered, blonde-haired, blue-eyed surfer boy.

Before jumping out of the front seat, we pledged to write letters to each other to keep our friendship alive, a seventeen-year-old boy and a thirteen-and-a-half-year-old girl.

I ran inside after waving Mark off in the darkness. The happiness I felt was overwhelming. I hadn't looked forward to this holiday, yet here I was smiling the happiest smile ever after a period when life had kept taking from me, crippling me. I felt alive. Words could not describe my feelings.

As I ran inside the front door, I heard laughter and conversation coming from the kitchen.

Zsstt...zsstt....

I sat on the chair next to my mother. I noticed many empty beer stubbies and full ashtrays scattered across the small, round dining table. The laughter dwindled as the conversation shifted to my least favourite person, Bertie the Bee, and how good a workmate he had been to Tim. My father, always ready to disagree, did so with his volume turned too high. Tim shared stories of good times with Bertie the Bee, while my father recounted not-so-great moments. Both men were now competing for the best or worst story about my least favourite person.

Voices escalated with growing hostility. I was glad when
Molly quickly wound up the socialising in the kitchen.
We each said good night and went to bed. I found it
hard to fall asleep, as I lay thinking of Mark, his friends,
skating, and the circus. Eventually, I drifted off to sleep.

I woke sometime later, abruptly afraid in the darkness
of the room where I had slept the previous nights. I felt
uncomfortable; something heavy and moving was in my
bed. Scared, I realised it was the sweaty body of Tim, his
beer gut pressed against me, his stinking breath in my
face, his whiskers scraping my cheek. He edged closer
into my bed beside me.

I slowly grabbed the sheets tightly and pulled them
between us, but he pulled them away. "Stop," I whispered.

But he shushed me; I could smell his repulsive breath
again. He pulled my hands towards his body and
wriggled closer to me, then grabbed at my pyjamas.

His breath…

He was pulling at my legs.

He was tearing at my clothes.

I was whispering, "No," as loudly as I could.

His wet, sweaty hands were clumsy as they grabbed parts
of me.

"Be quiet," said the voice of Tim.

Stifled breathing. I was terrified.

He had much more strength than I did.

I stopped fighting. Terrified, I became voiceless. I'd struggled against his weight, sweat, and power, but he won. Then it was over. He looked into my eyes for the last time, then grazed his whiskers against my cheek as he clumsily wriggled off me and out of the bed, then left. As I held my breath, I realised I was floating into numbness again.

I lay awake staring at the darkness of the ceiling that night, the nausea stirring in my gut. Numbness meant I could not think inside my head, yet I felt the sickness stirring in my stomach. The hamster wheel was churning. Again.

Was there a safe place for me in this life, my own actual life? I was exhausted from it all, from every single thing.

When the morning light rose, I remained fatigued and frozen with fear. I was petrified at the thought of facing him. What was I going to do, or say? Who was I going to tell, and when? Could I do any of the things I so badly wanted to do, yet was also too frightened to do?

My parents were beaming as they hugged Molly and Tim. They were overflowing with gratitude and praise for the generous gestures of Tim and Molly as we prepared to leave our holiday hellhole. As was expected, I gave Tim and Molly a quick good-bye peck on the cheek and said a gracious thank you. Fake. I then made a run for our car.

Unsent Letter

Dear Me

Do you know numb bodies can still run!

-24-
Madder than Hell

On the long drive back home, drowsiness fought with a wave of new emotions. The car hummed steadily along the road, a stark contrast to the unrest that brewed within me. Looking out of the window at the passing landscape, I sensed changes stirring inside me. There was a certain peace in the scenery, yet I couldn't shake off the nervousness of impending disturbance, like a calm before a storm. A deep anger surfaced within me, intense and profound, akin to the rage I had witnessed in my father, sharp and unpredictable. I felt nauseous, but not enough to stop my mind from circling Tim. This time, the harm was not from my father, but a stranger. My thoughts replayed the sly intrusion of a man into my safe space, his calculated intention, his violation, and my helplessness.

And I was madder than hell.

Confusion mixed with rage. I wanted to scream, yell, and lash out at the car window, my pillow, the sun, the moon, anything that would not fight back. The fury felt unnatural, yet at the same time both necessary and oddly comforting, even as it unsettled me.

That night, as our car pulled into our garage, I showered as soon as possible. Then, I did so repeatedly over the next few days, scrubbing the man and memory from the inside and outside of my body. Unfortunately, I couldn't scour away the stench of the memory of the deviant.

The smell of alcohol gripped my attention even more. Whenever it lingered, he haunted my thoughts for days and nights.

In the following weeks, I deliberately avoided my father to escape further conflicts; one more blow would break me. The anger I carried made me wary, afraid I might explode if he provoked me. My body roiled with anxiety. I stared blankly, had no appetite, was deaf to sound, and found nothing around me worthy of notice. My inner world dulled and became isolated.

My anger simmered over time, swelling into a fierce, searing flame. Soon, my inner ache followed: then tears. I cried uncontrollably, the intensity leaving me physically hurting. My emotions swung from rage to overwhelming sorrow.

I wanted to scream my truth to my father and mother, desperate for them to understand what had happened. Fear held me back, silencing the words I needed to say, so Tim's violation haunted me, my tears a constant reminder that I could not stop crying until I released the secret to someone.

I was trained to be silent. But this time I wasn't. I broke the training decree.

Eventually, I went to my mother, who was in the kitchen. Through my shame and embarrassment, I began telling her how I had suffered. Why had I suffered. How I held enormous hatred for Tim the deviant?

There was little reaction from my mother; she continued doing what she was doing, peeling pumpkin!

I stood beside her, waiting, staring at the floor, then looking at her face. Finally, her eyes raised to me, then back to the pumpkin. "I'll talk to Bertie," she said flatly.

I left the kitchen, sidestepped the bindies, and sat amongst the nasturtiums, dazed by exhaustion and emotional numbness. I didn't care anymore; I was too tired. Despite doubting my mother's promise to speak to Bertie, part of me felt relief. I had finally voiced my truth and was no longer holding the secret alone.

Within weeks, my mother told Bertie the Bee what Tim had secretly done to me in the night.

"Fuckin' liar," he spat angrily to my mother.

Bertie said I made up the story to hurt the family who had generously let us stay at their home, were incredibly hospitable and gave us a fantastic seaside holiday. How could I tell such lies?

I was a liar, and I wasn't to be believed!

I was ashamed. Embarrassed. Confused. And every other feeling associated with being invisible, unworthy, and useless.

Zsstt…that night, my mother drank alone in darkness, again.

I didn't sit beside her this time.

Tragically, I was blamed for igniting a spiteful family feud, a conflict that spread between my mother, Bertie the Bee, and Tim and Molly's whole family. My shame deepened as the fallout left me even more isolated and responsible.

The shame in my body was indescribable. My energy levels were depleted. I didn't care. I didn't have the fight left to care.

Once, I overheard my mother defend me, but my father stayed silent. I was called a slut. My mother let my abuse be ignored; her inaction was either a choice or a sign she couldn't endure the fight. I felt betrayed, my hope for protection shattered.

I was beaten. I broke. I gave in, again, the dirty-rotten-mongrel-bastard-kid. The slut.

Was I surprised not to have my parents' support? I was, yet should I have been, really?

One more perforation of my dignity. Of the girl, me. A violated body, shame-filled with more ache, more disgust, and more disabling anxiety.

My fateful experience with Tim, alongside the consequences of not being believed, heightened my awareness of my parents' care for me, which I calculated at 0.000.

As an adult, I came to recognise my father's own despair in his abuse because I now lived it. I began to understand the ruthless power inflicted when someone violates you. The betrayal, the helplessness…these scars last a lifetime. Sexual abuse and alcohol are a terrifying union.

Unfortunately, I also realised that to tell of violations to your body and soul is paralysing. To say out loud the words, 'He touched me. He hurt my body,' is so very difficult. I wonder why that is. Is it because the shame eats you up, and the wanting to be believed is so strong that the risk of not being believed stops you from saying anything?

Labelled a liar, even knowing I was not, consumed
chunks of my energy, but I had to remain upright. My
parents offered no comfort. I was left living in a body
that shook inside and a mind that worried about whether
or not I would be believed in every exchange. The fact
that my body was holding onto the fear, misery, and ache
was another lesson learned, but not for decades to come.

My being, my body, was used by my father for flogging
when he was in his full fury. Now, that same body had
been abused and touched for a different man's power
and pleasure. In those moments of darkness, I wondered
if anyone else heard the sheets rustling? If, somehow, my
silent cries carried beyond the confines of my mind. It was
an eerie thought that both comforted and terrified me; I
could be heard but also exposed. These reflections, brief
as they were, reminded me of my presence, my voice, even
amidst the violation.

Life throws moments at you that you cannot
comprehend! One moment, I was at a skating rink, with
joy, tenderness, and heartfelt connection with a beautiful
boy, and the very same night, in bed, the disgust of
alcohol and rape. There are no words yet invented from
the fifty-two letters in the alphabet to describe the feelings
I felt in that twenty-four-hour period.

Unsent Letter

Dirty Rotten Mongrel Bastard Tim,

I hope you come to visit me one day

I have a softball bat!

A Thorough Stupor

Still in a thorough stupor from being assaulted by the monstrous Tim, I felt a heaviness linger within me as our family repacked for our next holiday to Ari Bay. Returning to our regular holiday house and the sun and blue waters I loved, my mood shifted, especially once I found myself fishing from the old wooden jetty with our kid-sized rods, one of my favourite things to do in the calm waters off Ari Bay.

Our holidays at Ari Bay were always filled with long days of swimming in the clear waters and the rolling surf off The Point. Running along the white sand dunes, barbecues with friends while fighting off the millions of mosquitoes, and bingo games in the community hall were all the things that made the holiday fun. While there were plenty of screaming arguments, this time there were no beatings, making my body almost lighter, even in the midst of the chaos.

About three days in, I relaxed in the sun on the front yard grass with my friend Carly. Soon, a dust-covered car with three or four surfboards on top appeared around the corner and pulled up beside our fence. I stood to see who it was: Mark, my blue-eyed surfer boy, from the skating

rink, who came to the circus and with whom I pledged to
write letters. It was the most astonishing surprise!

I ran to him, and we hugged for a long time. Mark and
his friends, Mick and Andy, had driven from Sydney
to visit me at Ari Bay. We were ecstatic. Mark, Carly,
Mick, Andy, and I spent the next few days at the surfing
beaches, swimming and fishing at Ari Bay. We had
big family barbecues, talked, walked the beaches, and
laughed until my blue-eyed surfer boy and his friends
packed up and left for Sydney as quickly as they had
arrived. I felt charmed, as if under a spell! I recall only
good times, never-ending conversation, friendship, and
belonging. Mark's surprise visit, and the tenderness and
safety I felt with him, made this holiday the best.

While my heart was full of love and sunshine, I didn't
tell Mark about the deviant-in-my-bed thoughts that still
crowded my memories. We were young and respectful;
there was no need to share it, not yet. I also never
told Mark about my family's domestic abuse. Deeply
ashamed, I wouldn't risk him knowing about my family.

Our blue-water holiday soon ended.

We packed up and returned to 1-5-8 and our normal
routine. For a time after our holiday, I felt happy, trying
to dismiss memories of Tim, the feud, and the label of
liar. A few days later, I found a package from Mark in the
mailbox. Excited, I ran inside, read his letter, then opened
the package. Inside a maroon velvet box was a shining
yellow-and-white gold ring. I stared, held my breath, and
placed the ring on my finger, crying happy tears. I wished
Mark were there to see how much I loved the ring and to
know how much I appreciated his gift. I wore it proudly,
and I felt adored. The friendship ring meant so much
to me. It showed me that I was important and that my

parents loved me and I mattered. I felt stronger, as if I had an ally, and I gained a new focus and a real reason to live.

Writing to Mark gave me purpose and a way to express myself, helping me work through my mixture of feelings. His long, detailed letters gave me goosebumps. He wrote about his work, surfing, saving for a house, and other interesting aspects of his life. There were times I felt elated, almost unbearably so, knowing he was true to his word, unlike my parents, whom I didn't trust. Mark and I wrote and chatted for three years and visited each other a few times. It was extraordinary to visit Mark and his family in Sydney. Young love taught me:

- What the sense of adoration feels like

- The understanding of what "filled with love" means inside my body

- Those tender moments taught me responsibility in caring for another

- Which in turn taught me how to pay attention to myself

- Knowing that we both were equally important.

-26-

The Elephant in the Room

My parents started farming me out to families more often, and I still did not like it. The next adventure was for four weeks. I was farmed out to other families for four weeks, not seeing my parents for that time. They got their way again. I was sent to stay with Bobby, a friend of my mother's, and her daughter, Jennifer. Jennifer and I attended the same school, although we didn't know each other well, aside from having played in the same netball team the previous year.

Living with Bobby and Jennifer for four weeks was like a holiday in downtown City Central. Jennifer and I had complete freedom to do whatever we wanted.

My very first drug and alcohol experiment happened in that house. I went to my first grown-up party before walking back to Jennifer's in the early morning hours, after drinking something that made me awfully bloody sick. We went to mid-week, dark, dim house parties in dirty, dusty houses where smoke hung heavily in the air, which scared the hell out of me.

We mingled. It was my first time mingling with people who were into each other in a big way, like nakedly significant ways, in lounge rooms and bedrooms. This was another world; it was an unfamiliar world of drugs and strange faces and bodies mixed with the familiarity of alcohol overload and sleepless nights.

My world of risk-taking became scarier than 1-5-8 Lavandar Avenue, and I was more afraid than I'd ever been. Living scared for as long as I could remember, in fear almost every day, I'd become a risk taker, without even knowing it. I'd risked behaviours to stand up to my father and to escape life-threatening floggings.

I was now living without parents, and I was in charge of myself. I faced frightening situations, walking through self-exacting fires. I chose to live a life of risk-taking and accepted the double dread as my norm! And I was only fourteen years old.

My new friend Jennifer acted like an adult, and I thought she was awesome. She cooked her own meals, did her own washing, and did what she wanted without asking. She was someone who received a lot of attention from her friends because she was confident. That's what Jennifer told me, anyway, so I wanted to be just like her.

The next highlight of freedom was Tuesday night in a city nightclub.

As young, unattended, naive, and excited teenage girls, we dressed in cork wedge heels, hot pants, and sequinned T-shirts and caught the 6.45pm bus. I didn't know what else to expect from a nightclub except that the whole night was going to be "unreal", so cool.

I knew there would be drinking and a DJ, but I quickly discovered that wasn't all that went on in a nightclub. Jennifer and I both passed the front-door security guard without any problems. We walked straight to the bar.

Leaning on the bar, I looked at the numerous bottles of spirits on the wall. I realised I didn't know what any of those bottles contained or what I was supposed to drink. I wasn't going to drink beer like my mother, so I stared at the bottles. Some were pretty colours, and I was going to choose a coloured drink, but I didn't know how to order. So I had the same drink as Jennifer, a completely bloody horrible Scotch and Dry, but I drank it to fit in.

As I sipped the brownish poison from my glass, my determination grew to fit into this new world; this free life I would live with Jennifer for three more weeks! I would make myself fit in and make friends. I was about to embark on new and scary experiences, but despite my fears, I was determined to choose what I wanted to do with my newfound freedom alongside my friend.

I continued writing to Mark, went to school, went to nightclubs, lived without floggings or forced feeding, and made choices about what I wanted.

That Tuesday night, we danced, and we sang to the DJ's songs, and we laughed so much. I had to remind myself repeatedly that night that I was free.

At 11pm, we walked to the lift together; well, not exactly. Jennifer was wrapped around a bloke named Jon. I thought we were being driven home to her place in his big flashy car, which he mentioned in the lift, but we weren't. We pulled into a driveway somewhere I'd never been. The engine was turned off, and we all got out of the car.

It was his place. It was about 11.30pm by now, so I guessed there would be no school again tomorrow. The long-haired, handsome bloke led us inside his quirky boho place and offered us a cup of hot Milo while we chatted and got comfy on his soft, cushion-filled lounge.

He appeared kind and pleasant enough as he washed our cups, then showed me to the bedroom where I was to sleep for the night.

Holy hell. Was I now having sleepovers at my new friend's new boyfriend's house?

I wasn't entirely comfortable, especially after my Tim experience, but, hey, I'd been doing uncomfortable for the last fourteen years. What was new?

I would be okay, I told myself. I was safe with Jennifer. I had my own room with my own double bed. I had been made a lovely hot Milo, and he even washed my cup! I was going to sleep in my underwear and shut the bedroom door. What was the big deal? Why was I worrying?

I closed the door, got undressed, and then the house was quiet. I jumped under the covers, and I fell asleep within minutes. Well, that's how it felt when I was woken from my sleep.

I woke to a heavy weight on me, pressing me down. I moved my hands towards the weight as I opened my eyes, startled to see a body straddling mine, a hand pressing heavily over my mouth. My breath stopped as I looked up into the eyes of the man, the Milo maker, who had shown me to the spare bedroom. His eyes were like steel, shiny and boring holes through mine. I was frozen with fear, just like when I saw Tim's face. I was reliving the same nightmare.

This time, though, it was Jon. His body was stiff, heavy on me. Naked except for a tiny white elephant costume over his erection. He pointed to the ears of the elephant as they sat against his body, while the trunk stood stiffly. I lay still as he joked about it. He grabbed both of my arms and held them up over my head against the wooden bedhead. I couldn't catch my breath and screamed out in fear. He grabbed my face, hard.

"Shut up," he whispered angrily.

I grabbed at him, but I couldn't move my arms under his strength. He leaned forward, using all his might against me. He was smiling as he emerged victorious from the struggle. It terrified me, another madman in my presence.

I was screaming inside and felt trapped under his weight, my arms held tightly together.

"Let go," I told him through clenched teeth, feeling like my anger and fear could explode inside of me.

His face came close to mine as he let go of my arms, gripping both hands around my throat, threatening to tighten if I didn't shut up.

Inside, I was raging, and I hit him impulsively with both free hands. His grip tightened, and I immediately feared I was truly under threat of strangulation as he held his hands on my throat, glaring at me.

"Don't move," he commanded in his intoxicated state, as he slowly removed his hands from my throat, letting me breathe more freely. He pushed and pulled at my clothing in all directions, heavy and awkward, sliding over me. I wanted to scream and hit him again, but I didn't. I wanted to do all those things at once, but then I froze.

He faced me and stared again, threatening me. Petrified, I believed he would strangle me again. I lay as still as I could. My head hit the headboard as he lurched again and again. It hurt everywhere he touched me; everywhere. I hoped my friend didn't hear, and I hoped she did.

Nobody appeared at the bedroom door, so she didn't. His sweat, breath, and power game nauseated me.

I fought hard against Jon, trying to stop the penetration of my soul and body, wanting to hit out and scream again, but I didn't. He won, victorious in the fight with his promise of strangulation if I didn't allow him access to my body.

He then fell heavily on me, his drunk, limp, lifeless body lying on top of my own frightened, limp, lifeless body. He lay there for a long time, his sweat mixing with mine or my tears; I couldn't tell which was which as the wetness of whatever it was slid over the fear and racing pulse he had created inside me. I could feel the fear and anger still raging inside. I eventually found the courage and strength to roll him off me.

He suddenly came back to life; he sat up quickly. "Shut up, be quiet. You asked for this, you little slut. You say a word, and I'll tell Jennifer you asked for this."

I lay there for the rest of the night, staring at the ceiling, feeling him still on, in and around me. My head still ached. Nausea roiled in my gut from the wheel churning; I thought I was going to be sick! I sat up all night, leaning against the pillows and staring at the wall!

My head was a mix of visions; pushing, sweat, and holding me down…everything, visions of everything.

Why was this happening to me? Why did men take this from me, from my body? What was I doing wrong for this to happen to me? Again!

Hours later, the sun began to rise, and I finally heard Jennifer making a telephone call from somewhere outside my bedroom door. Ten minutes later, a taxi arrived.

Jennifer and I returned to her place, both tired and silent for most of the day, having showered and slept for most of it. I showered for a long time to wash away the violation, the disgust, the sweat, and the memory of the friendly, Milo-making Jon, the intoxicated, violent rapist!

No school for two more days. Not long to go at this house before I headed back to my own house. I wasn't staying here. It was safer at 1-5-8. The violence of beatings was better than the violence of rape!

-27-

Exasperations

Saturday morning arrived, so I wasn't guilty about missing school. We had a casual day planned. A friend was coming over for girl talk.

Telling Jennifer about her boyfriend's action was deeply worrying, but I made the hard decision; this was a good day to do it.

Enough time had lapsed, giving me space to think, and now I felt able to speak about it, kind of. Anyway, there were three of us to discuss the whole frightening matter, which was better than telling Jennifer about her boyfriend on my own.

It was about 11am, and we were all still sitting in the bedroom, my thoughts racing and my gut somersaulting when I took a deep breath to say the words aloud, readying myself to feel her pain and my shame!

"Jennifer...I want to tell you something."

I began slowly, trying to tell her what happened, then one million words spilled out of my mouth like a torrent of water, letting her know what happened from when Jon showed me my bedroom until he left me after his threats.

I told her about his total disregard for my saying no.
I told her how frightened I was as I fought him off,
how he grabbed me by the throat and threatened real
strangulation. I cried through the recount of my fear for
my life, the nausea, the violation, and the demoralising,
aggressive rape.

I was crying. I was shaking. I showed her the bruising
on my thigh where he had grabbed me. I felt humiliated,
and let her know how scared I felt to tell her about being
raped, especially by her boyfriend!

Above all, in my fight for myself, I needed to be heard
and believed!

And my truth came out exactly right, exactly as it
happened.

Jennifer's face, mid-story, turned paler shades of white! At
the story's end, slowly, she got to her feet, then threw her
arms around, infuriated. She planted them heavily on her
hips, totally exasperated by my story. Stomping back and
forth across the bedroom, angry as all hell, Jennifer did
not look at me.

After a good hundred-meter walk, she looked up at me.
"You know Jon would never do that," she yelled. "You
made up this whole story because you were asking him
for it."

I was as humiliated as I imagined I would be if she didn't
believe me and a whole lot more! "I don't know him,
Jennifer, that's the thing. We stayed at his place because
you took me there. I didn't ask to stay there!"

I told Jennifer, as she stared at me, that everything I had
said was true! I wasn't asking him for anything. I slept in
a bed in a house she took me to! I was not anywhere near

her boyfriend. She saw me go to bed, so how could I be near him? I was furious as all hell myself by now!

I told Jennifer straight up that I wouldn't have sex with her boyfriend; she was my friend first, and I wasn't drunk. He was, and it was rape. How pathetic this demeaning back-and-forth made me feel. She had no compassion for me, no belief or trust in my account. Was I wearing a sign, visible to others but invisible to me, that said, "You can crash and burn this girl; she is here for your pleasure, your yearning, and her pain?" That's exactly how I felt. What was I doing to men I didn't know that made them violate me?

Jennifer took a while to respond, still marching back and forth in the bedroom. Then Jennifer spoke up, calling me a tramp!

Then she let me know I wasn't to speak to her for the rest of my time at her place.

That would be easy. In a very short time, I would be back in the hell of 1-5-8! Paradise by comparison to living with Jennifer!

The next time Jennifer spoke to me was a few days later at school, when she stopped by during morning tea break to tell me how shocked she was that I had sex with her boyfriend. Jennifer said she didn't ever want to see me again, ever, and we were no longer friends. I was unsurprised!

And that felt like the end of my friendship with Jennifer, but it did not end there. A week later, as she swanned past me at school after our "I never want to see you again" talk, Jennifer told me to expect nothing more from Mark, my blue-eyed surfer boy. To my utter astonishment, Jennifer let me know she'd contacted Mark to tell him I was having sex with her boyfriend, that I was untrustworthy, and that he should dump me!

I went into an internal meltdown and an external freeze!

I cared, and I didn't! I wanted to cry, and I didn't! I wanted to run away, and, again, I didn't!

The saddest of all is what I did! Instead of doing anything to make me feel better or to save me from more torment, I begged her to believe me! "Your boyfriend raped me. He strangled me, threatening more if I didn't stay quiet! But I didn't. I told you. Why would you believe him and not me?"

She put on a stupid teenage girl "I hate you" face and marched off.

I was gutted; no words could precisely capture the agonising misery and heartbreak I endured over the next few months. I felt like I had lost both a girlfriend and a tender boyfriend in one moment, the result of a single lie by one exceedingly desperate, seemingly insecure girl and a rapist; people who used me to sidestep their own lives of emptiness. Of course, I eventually realised it was no loss at all in my own world. I was now free from two people I had never invited into my life, who had been thrust into it by unexpected events, and were now both out of it!

Yet still, I was the person suffering with the pain and shame in the blame game. This situation took a while to overcome, as teenage life events often do. I survived the horror and heartbreak of my life at that time and got up and kept on going.

I didn't tell my parents about the rape or about what Jennifer said to Mark, nor did I tell anybody else.

And to be very clear, I never saw or spoke to Jennifer again.

I did speak to Mark, but I explained the situation in a roundabout way. I didn't call it rape because I was too ashamed. He was upset to hear I had slept with someone, but for some reason, he let that misdemeanour go, and for some reason, I let the truth slip by too.

Can you believe I lived for scores of years, allowing myself to appear as a girl who was unfaithful to her boyfriend, whom she adored! That was how deeply indoctrinated I was in my lack of worth, raised as I was by my parents. I allowed my first real boyfriend to think I was unfaithful because I was too ashamed to speak up, to say the word rape, and explain the circumstances! I had been sexually violated and raped twice in the first two years of knowing Mark. The shame surrounding those circumstances was so deep, heavy, and suffocating that I could not allow myself to say the words out loud, so I never told him.

The long-distance romance with my surfer boy lasted even through that disaster!

Then, eventually, our love lost its once hope-filled story, with letters and contact becoming less frequent. The love stories have evolved into beautiful, treasured memories of puppy love's innocence, with the gentle, beautiful Billy and the tenderness and love of Mark, a glorious, charming boy, both of whom remain precious and treasured as meaningful relationships in my life.

The long-lasting impact of knowing Billy and Mark as I did, and of course, of teacher Harry Watson having my back at school, distanced me from my secret life of fear and agony, as did my friendships with my girlfriends, Carol, Debbie, Lana, and Ann. My primary school and early teenage years taught me to understand the value and significance of experiences of love and friendship in a way no other lessons have.

-28-

The Hoppers

I was twelve. I know that for sure because one of the outfits I was given around that time was a cream shirt and brown corduroy jeans, and I wore that exact outfit on a trip to Sydney.

Every couple of months, I would come home from school to find the laundry filled with things I didn't recognise. Not messy-full, but deliberately full. Stereos, plural. Televisions, plural. And about six gigantic suitcases, all packed tight with things that didn't belong to us, yet were suddenly living in our house.

I'd watch my parents unpack watches, shirts, trousers, shoes, hats, and suits. Good things. New things. Too many things. The leather on the boots smelled strong, stiff, and new. The shirts' fabrics were crisp, almost smelling of chemicals, and I could feel the texture of the collars, the soft lining of the jackets, the stiff folds of the suits. I ran my fingers over the hems and buttons like a child exploring treasure.

I never asked a question.

They just appeared.

I never saw the goods arrive. I never saw them leave.

Even now, that detail nags at me. These weren't small items. They were old seventies stereos, heavy, boxed. Big televisions with thick backs and glass screens. Multiple overstuffed suitcases.

They would have needed a truck.

Someone would have had to carry them in. Someone would have had to carry them out. It couldn't have been quiet. It couldn't have been subtle.

Did anyone see them come? Did anyone see them go?

I still don't know.

Sometimes I imagine a large truck rumbling up the street, the tires crunching gravel, someone heaving boxes into our laundry while the neighbours look the other way. I wonder who would have known about it. Who was part of this strange rhythm of deliveries and disappearances? I was always a dot connector, even as a child, and this is one dot that has never quite made sense.

One afternoon, I came home from school and found a five-foot white freezer sitting in the lounge room. Massive. Impossible to miss. It didn't fit anywhere else. I never saw it come either. It was just there, like it had always belonged. The metal was cold to the touch when I gingerly ran my hand along it, and the handle was smooth and slick under my palm. The smell of cold and plastic filled the lounge, a strange, sterile scent that lingered long after I left it alone.

I tried to make sense of things the only way a child can. We didn't have much money, so I assumed my parents must have come into some. A bonus. A lucky break. Something grown-up and financial that I still didn't understand.

The suitcases were the strangest part.

Sometimes my parents would call me in and say it casually, as if it were normal: "Try this on. Here's a pair of jeans. Here's a pair of cords. Here's a jumper. Here are some sand shoes. Do you like this sloppy joe?"

And I did. I always did.

That was how I got clothes, not from shops or by choice, but by being fitted like a mannequin pulled from storage. I was grateful, because gratitude was expected.

But I noticed things.

Some suits would fit a big man with a forty-two-inch chest, then smaller ones. Oversized jackets. Smaller jackets. Big hats. Small hats. Big shoes. Small shoes. Ties in every colour. None of it matched the people living in our house.

I remember asking once, confused more than suspicious: "Why have you got all these? Who are they for?" I remember the scratch of the fabric under my fingertips, the heaviness of the jackets in my hands, the smooth leather of the shoes, the cold metal of the zipper teeth on the trousers.

My parents didn't answer.

Much later, my mother would say, "Oh, the Hoppers bring them to us."

The Hoppers?

I didn't know what that meant, and I didn't ask. In our house, you accepted explanations even when they explained nothing. Pretending. Always pretending.

Observing. Connecting dots silently, because asking too many questions was dangerous in small ways that you learned to respect.

Then one night, not long after the freezer appeared, I woke up with that heavy, wrong feeling, the one that tells you someone is in the house when they shouldn't be.

I was terrified.

So, the sounds of the house at night became magnified. Every floorboard squeak echoed down the narrow hall, and the faint hum of the refrigerator sounded like a warning siren. My pulse thudded in my ears. I called out and ran from my room. My mother ran out, too. Everything felt loud, fast, and panicked, with feet on the floor, voices raised, hearts racing. We were really, really scared.

My father told us to go back to bed.

That was it.

No explanation. No reassurance. No anger. No attempt to stop whoever was there. Just go back to bed.

We did.

The next morning, the freezer was gone.

Later that morning, I noticed marks on the carpet. 1-5-8 had one long, narrow hallway down one side of the house. There it was, a single drag line pressed deep into the pile, running straight along it to the carport doorway. You could see exactly where the freezer had been dragged. I traced it with my finger, pressing into the fibres, feeling the imprint left behind. My stomach twists at the memory, even decades later.

At the time, I didn't understand what it meant. I only knew that someone had been in our house, that my mother and I had been terrified, and that the person who was meant to protect us had done nothing much to ease our terror.

From that night forward, sleep was never sleep again. Every sound carried significance. Every creak, every unfamiliar noise felt like a threat. I lay awake, tense, listening, waiting. The house seemed to breathe differently. Shadows moved faster than they should. When the person who is supposed to protect you responds to danger with silence, your body learns a new rule: you are on your own.

That lesson stayed long after the freezer was gone.

Fifty years later, I was talking online with a student I'd gone to primary school with, on the school reunion page. Names resurfaced. Histories crossed again. He told me he'd ended up working in the same environment as my father.

Then, casually, jokingly, he said something that finally made sense of this memorable moment of my childhood.

He talked about buying all kinds of stuff from my father at his workplace. I didn't understand, of course, until he mentioned suitcases, clothes, stereos, and televisions. My father would store them in a big shed for only a couple of days, during which staff were invited to purchase them at a low price for forty-eight hours.

Sell them.

I asked about the freezer, the one that had been in our house, for about three or four days.

He said, "What do you mean? You lost a freezer?"

That was the moment everything lined up.

All those years of suitcases. The stereos. The televisions. The freezer that appeared and disappeared. The clothes I wore with quiet gratitude. The questions I never learned to ask.

My home hadn't just been a home.

It had been a storage unit.

And I was twelve years old, living inside it.

Unsent Letter

Unsurprised am I

So sad and ashamed, I am

-29-

A History Lesson in Bad Ideas

Spending a weekend at sunny Ari Bay was perfectly timed after my traumatising experience with Jennifer and Jon. I was in a state of internally demonising them and myself. I felt I needed a new environment where I could be carefree, swim, fish, sing, dance, and relax.

However, not all was well, as the brothers of bad ideas were staying in a cottage on the property. A Saturday night barbecue was arranged, and both arrived on time. I concentrated on the good stuff: friends, the glorious fire pit with dancing flames and embers, and the fact that we were at Ari Bay for the weekend.

Sam the Fizz came into the kitchen to chat while my mother and I prepared the salads to serve with the barbecued steaks. He slurred his words as he told us about his fishing days with his mates on Ari Bay and how he'd recently retired. He loved the time he spent with the new mates he had made on the island.

I didn't trust him one bit, waiting for him to grab me to pull me onto his lap and hold on tightly, just like Bertie the Bee.

Sam the Fizz said he'd invited some friends to our barbecue, who'd be along soon. We chatted about his fishing that morning, but it wasn't a good story, so there wouldn't be fresh Ari Bay-caught fish for our barbecue.

Salads were prepared, and as I took them outside to the dinner tables, I saw Sam near the front fence, waiting for his friends to arrive. Sure enough, as soon as I was back inside the kitchen gathering cutlery and bread rolls, Sam came with a nod and a smile.

Bertie the Bee had the barbecue underway outside. The spotlights were on, and we had at least three mosquito sprays ready for the visitors. Two mosquito coils were burning, keeping millions of mosquitoes at bay. Meanwhile, my mother and I had organised the remaining food. I still hadn't noticed any new faces in the kitchen or through the window overlooking the big yard outside. However, I guessed that Sam had said his friends had arrived, so we went ahead and served the barbecue feast.

Sam the Fizz continued to swig from his beer bottle and called to me, "My mates are in the kitchen, wanna meet 'em?" He gave a huge grin!

"Yeah, sure!" I said, not quite telling the truth!

Sitting on a chair near the door at the kitchen table, Sam the Fizz sat next to me.

"Here they are," he said, rolling up the sleeve of his flannelette shirt.

I looked at him, then towards the door! I didn't understand; since nobody else was in the kitchen, I waited, but no one appeared. As Sam the Fizz continued rolling up his sleeve, I heard him say, "Here he is." I looked at his sleeve to see the head of a snake poking out! I gasped and sat very still.

"I brought his mate with him," said Sam, rolling the other sleeve higher. Out popped the speckled brown head of another snake he had wrapped around his arm. I stared at Sam the Fizz without moving a muscle, waiting for him to do something even more stupid with the snakes, but he didn't move either. Thank goodness my mother came into the kitchen, looking for both me and Sam the Fizz. She saw the worry in my eyes and asked if I was okay. My look told her I wasn't. She stared at Sam and the two snakes wrapped around his right arm, held in place by the tight flannelette sleeve.

"Sam, don't be such an idiot," she said, "get rid of those snakes. You know she doesn't like snakes."

"Don't be like that. They're my mates. I brought 'em with me for dinner. They won't hurt anyone."

"Get rid of those snakes now, and don't let me see them around this house again! Go on, now!" said my mother in a tone and manner I was not used to!

Of course, Sam the Fizz didn't. Not right away.

He took his time, looking at me, then at my mother, as if she'd gone full military rank. It was as if we shouldn't be frightened of two snakes in our kitchen. He thought we were ridiculous for being frightened by two snakes wrapped around his drunk arm. Sam made out that there was something wrong with us and nothing wrong with him for bringing snakes into a house.

This was before he checked if everybody was okay with snakes being brought into their house!

My brain bent out of shape. It really did, and it hurt.

I watched as Sam looked at my mother, then slowly rolled down his flannelette shirt sleeves, buttoned the cuffs, and walked outside. My mother didn't trust Sam at all, so she called after him to make sure those snakes were let loose way down the back of the yard, in the corner where nobody ever went. I went outside as far as the barbecue, but my eyes kept following Sam as he walked down the back of the yard and over to the corner of the fence line. I saw him let the snakes go in the darkness, bending down to release them onto the grass. I felt such relief.

I had been looking forward to our delicious barbecue dinner, but after watching the snakes being released, I lost my appetite. Sam the Fizz returned to the barbecue table, rushing to fill his plate like he was a starving man missing his mates!

I couldn't handle being in the darkness for the rest of the night. I was scared Sam the Fizz hadn't released the snakes. How do you trust a drunk man who thinks it's funny to bring snakes to a family barbecue?

I didn't sit at the barbecue table with the rest of the group that night; I stood. All the while, I watched the ground around me closely to make sure I was safe from the creepy, cold, slithery snakes.

Each rustling sound caught my attention, and I stared with intent, around the whole grounds to be sure there was no snake coming towards me. I, the child already freaked out by life, felt so terrified that I could not relax.

Finally, everyone left our barbecue, and my mother and I cleaned up, and then went to bed, exhausted. It was a hot night, so I didn't need to use my sleeping bag, even as a sheet.

The bedroom windows were opened, and though thousands of mosquitoes would come inside, I knew mosquito spray and coils would help keep them from stinging me and, hopefully, from buzzing in my ears. I climbed up to the top bunk and pushed the rolled-up sleeping bag to the end of my bed.

Punching my pillow, making it the perfect shape, I settled down, with my spirits up, trying to forget about the snakes and Sam the Fizz.

Unsent Letter

Dear Me,

Tear up the contract for the current family friends named

Bertie the Bee, Sam the Fizz, and Penny the Prickle.

Begin interviews for new family friends who do not

have a history of bad ideas.

-30-
Bagged

Sometime later, unsure if I was dreaming or actually awake, I was woken by the five-hundred-thousand mosquitoes buzzing around me. Their presence made me slide inside the sleeping bag. Too tired to do the job properly, I reached towards the bottom of the bed in the darkness. I unravelled the sleeping bag just enough to slide inside and pull it up over me, including my ears.

Comfort vanished; terror took its place. I froze with fright. I felt something scaly and cold inside, slithering and sliding over me and around me like it was racing to find an escape route. I froze, then screamed, then froze again.

I felt them, two snakes racing from the bottom of my sleeping bag, across and around me, scrambling to get out. Over my body, along and off the bed, and...I leapt out, shrieking for my mother.

Sam the Fizz ran inside, hearing my screams. He wondered out loud what was happening, but he already knew. I was so frightened that I was in a daze. Screaming hysterically, I didn't want to put my feet on the ground. So I stood on top of the kitchen table, screaming and jumping up and down, running in place, throwing my arms about, and looking around.

"Turn the lights on! Turn the lights on! My God, the snakes were inside my sleeping bag, Mum. They're still in here somewhere. The snakes are in here. Please help me. Mum, where are they? MUM."

Sam searched under beds, in beds, and everywhere in the house, but couldn't find the two snakes.

"They must've gone to the backyard," he said. "They won't hurt you. Don't worry, they won't come back."

"You-put-those-snakes-in-my-sleeping-bag!" I screamed, shocked.

"Just a game, kid," Sam the Fizz laughed stupidly.

"You idiot," my mother yelled. "Why would you do that? You know she's scared of snakes."

"It was just a joke; I didn't mean to upset anyone."

"Stop doing stupid things," my mother demanded.

I sat at the table for much of the night because I refused to go back into the bedroom. I wouldn't even pack my clothes to leave. I stayed on top of the table, watching every movement in the house. I had completely lost my mind and could think of nothing else but the terror of snakes slithering over and around my body in the dark, trapped in my sleeping bag. Fear sent me into a state of unreserved shock.

I was absolutely petrified. My body started at any sound. My mind kept replaying the vision. My breath came fast. I couldn't hear a word that was meant to calm me. I was captive to fear, panic, anger, and Sam the Fizz's stupidity. If I hated alcohol before, I hated it even more now.

Fear, lack of safety, lack of trust, and trauma had finally caught up with me. I could not take any more. My body collapsed.

In my world, alcohol made people do the stupidest things. It made them commit crimes and hurt others. It left people terrified, beaten, and even killed. I wanted to divorce my family. I wanted to un-friend Sam the Fizz. I could only trust a few relatives: my cousins, their parents, and my friends. I was divorcing Sam. I so wanted to sack him, never allowing him near me or my life again. I didn't think I could survive much longer with these people.

We were the great, indisputable family of strife in Brisbane: it was me versus bindies, me versus boredom, me versus my father's temper, and me versus Sam. Every day was a struggle for survival in this family with a majestic history of bad ideas.

Nightmares became part of my sleepless nights after that terrifying night. I was told not to be a sook. I was offered neither comfort nor conversation about the snakes. No one helped when I searched under beds for snakes at home. I had no shoulder to lean on when I couldn't sleep at night, worrying about snakes in my bed. No one expressed concern for my bad dreams about snakes, either.

It was just one more baffling event in the madness of my family. I learned to live with growing fear. Fear became more frequent, more normal for me, living in my body, in my family, in my lifetime.

Unsent Letter

Dear Anybody who will listen, Help me, please!

-31-

The Addict Apparent

Fear continued to follow me everywhere in my everyday life. At least, by then, my mother had promised to leave my father for good. Looking back, I realise fear became a default companion, shaping my responses. It taught me to be hypervigilant, making it hard to trust others, even when I wanted to. Yet, from today's perspective, I see it also forced me to become resilient and find strength in survival. Fear sculpted the boundaries of my world, pressing me into a sharper version of myself. My mother finally moved out and took me with her, away from my father. Unfortunately, he was still not out of our lives.

We lived in a small, dark, depressing unit not far from 1-5-8. Its affordability dictated our move.

I was attending school, and though life was better and more peaceful in some ways, it came at a cost. There was a new set of depressing circumstances. It was hard work, both financially and emotionally. My mother was drinking more than usual, making meaningful conversations almost impossible. She still liked to sit alone in the darkness and drink.

There were more zsstt sounds than ever. The situation weighed on me, so I decided to contribute financially. I left school at fifteen to find a job.

My mother enjoyed her job, yet was not entirely happy living alone and being the breadwinner in a small, dark unit.

Luckily for me, I found work almost right away. At just fifteen, I started as a receptionist in an architect's office near our place. The boss was a tall, wide woman who wore black clothes and large black glasses, with a short black bob and a very short, silly-looking fringe.

Winning the receptionist role at this workplace was an exciting opportunity, and I was thrilled to have a job that would help cover my living expenses. During my first week, I answered phones, scheduled appointments, and distributed mail. I felt grown-up. Payday was every Friday, and I was excited to receive my first paycheque.

The boss, who was wearing black clothing and had big black glasses, told me that the business hadn't earned enough money that week, so I wasn't able to be paid.

I raised my eyebrows at her, not faking it.

I told my mother about this. No response.

During the second week, my duties increased as I answered the phones, opened the mail for distribution, and began typing letters to clients. At first, I enjoyed the work immensely, feeling proud and eager. But Friday afternoon arrived, and my boss, wearing black glasses and sporting a very short, silly fringe, told me once again that the business hadn't earned much money that week so that she couldn't pay me again.

My initial excitement gave way to anxiety and distrust. I felt a knot of anxiety tighten in my stomach as I realised this wasn't just bad luck; I was being exploited, and I knew it. This was not the norm, and her justification felt increasingly manipulative with each passing week. I thought, I'm taking a lot of calls, your staff are busy, and I think you're lying.

I was unable to pay my mother's rent yet again. I was still asking her for money to cover public transportation costs for commuting to and from work. I explained to my mother why I wasn't being paid. I felt embarrassed explaining the missed payday, but my mother never commented on it. Still, from her expression, I could tell she wasn't happy with the situation.

Zsstt…zsstt….

Over the next four weeks, every Friday, the boss repeated her spiel about not being able to pay me. "I'm working on it," she said.

"Okay," was the last word I spoke to her.

When I arrived home, however, my mother didn't greet me in the same calm manner as she had over the past weeks.

"Mum, the boss didn't pay me again. She told me again that she's working on it, working on getting me paid. She can't pay me now," I said in a sarcastic voice mimicking the boss's tone.

Afraid, I apologised to my mother for not being able to pay rent again. I complained about the boss, the workload, and insisted I wasn't being paid. I was sure the boss wasn't honest about my wages.

"You're a liar," spat my mother angrily. "You're buying marijuana. You are being paid, and you're buying drugs. You're-a-liar-you-are-being-paid-and-you're-buying-drugs."

My throat closed like a fist, tightening with each syllable. I felt pressure in my chest, as though my ribs were caving in and squeezing my heart.

My mother kept repeating this accusation as she drank more that evening. Earlier, her words had stung, but as her speech grew slurred and she took longer to speak, I felt helpless. My mother was very drunk, and the more she drank, the less hope I had of changing her mind or reaching her.

I wasn't a liar or spending money on drugs. I wasn't paid at all. I was caught between a dishonest boss and my disbelieving mother.

My mother's angst, and the atmosphere grew more intense.

Zsstt continued as she drank increasingly. By the time I spoke to my mother again, later that night, I was begging her to believe my story.

My mother, still enraged, stormed into my bedroom and opened my drawers. Furiously, she began pulling my clothing out of my drawers, throwing them all on the floor.

"You're a liar. Get out," she said. "Get out of this house. You're on drugs. You're a drug addict. Get out of this house, liar."

My mother, drunk, then began throwing my clothes onto the lawn and yelling so loudly that the neighbours heard.

"Get out of my house, you drug addict. You'll not live here under my roof, you liar. Get out and don't come back."

I once again felt dissociated from my body and detached from my mother.

Trying to get through to my mother to tell her my truth about what was happening at work, in my first-ever job, was impossible. The same recording of her voice came back at me: I was a liar; I was buying drugs; and I needed to get out and never come back.

I was just fifteen years old, with a brain that was not working correctly at that moment, with zero money and no options for where to live. It was a late, dark, and cold night. My clothing was on the front lawn, and I was to leave home right then. An overwhelming sense of panic flooded me, then drained away, leaving me numb. Where was I to go? I could not think at the time. Numb had become normal, yet in that moment, I think I became even more numb, if that was possible.

I knelt on the front lawn, crying, overwhelmed by humiliation and shame as I packed my clothes into my school and softball bags. Despite feeling overwhelmed, I made a choice. I grabbed my softball bat first. It reminded me of my love for the game and the strength I found in it. The bat was a symbol of my resilience, something I controlled amid the chaos. With each item I gathered, I tried to cling to those fleeting pieces of agency, knowing I wasn't only a victim of my circumstances.

With my bags over both shoulders, I picked up my softball bat and glove and walked to the phone box on the corner, still in shock.

I called my best friend Carol collect. Her mother
answered, and I asked if I could stay in their home briefly,
since my mother had thrown me out of ours.

"It'll only be for a short time until I figure things out.
I have no money to give you. I'm sorry." I ran out of
words.

My insides rattled. I could barely speak from shock and
exhaustion. I felt drained, struggling to stay composed as
I called for help. Carol's mother asked me to wait while
she asked the family.

Waiting for that response felt like being deafened by
silence. I felt crippled by shame. It was, after all, a family
decision, and I was asking them for a place to live. The
embarrassment of knowing they were talking about me
was excruciating. I heard Carol's mother say something,
then another silence, and then, "Okay."

"Thank you so much. I'll be there sometime tonight. I'll
be there as soon as I can."

I began the walk. It was about an hour long, but I don't
remember much of it. I walked along the main roads,
my head down so no one would recognise me. I felt
embarrassed, as if I were an annoyance to everyone. I
wasn't sure why I was bothering my boss or my mother. I
couldn't understand why I was the problem!

I don't recall any details about arriving at Carol's place
that evening. I felt lost, alone, unloved, unlovable, lonely;
a nothing, a nobody who wasn't wanted because I wasn't.
That was a fact. My mother didn't want me.

I stayed with Carol's family for a few months. There was
laughter, fun, and loads of love, accompanied by cups
of tea, lively conversations, and music. In the mornings,

the smell of a delicious breakfast and brewed tea wafted through the house, while laughter echoed around the kitchen table. The evenings were filled with the vibrant notes of Carol's pianola, music that wrapped around me like a comforting blanket, pushing away the shadows of my past. There was music and singing. Often. They were the kind of family I wanted to have as my own. Kind, loving, funny, and generous, they treated me like one of their own.

I shared a bedroom with Carol, which was the most wonderful thing I experienced at the time. We chatted well into the night, singing and laughing as the best of friends do.

How colossally grateful I am to that family for taking me in when my mother wouldn't believe me because of a boss who wouldn't pay me.

How many genuine people in the world would do that for their daughter's friend? Doesn't that say so much about the value of friendship, especially in my case with Carol? It showed me how much her parents valued our friendship and what it meant to them. Carol and I shared the same wacky personality; we laughed at the same things; did the same silly things together; played her parents' pianola and sang at the top of our voices, weekend after weekend. Her parents never said a word about the noise. I didn't know whether the neighbours ever thought it was crazy times in that beautiful Queenslander, but we had the best of times. I was treated like a loved daughter, and it felt like magic to be in her home.

Thank you, Jesse, George, Niney, Linda, Alan, Peter, and Carol!

A few months later, my mother turned up, told me to pack my bags, and we left for a new home. As usual, I did as I was told, packed, and left.

I wasn't entirely unhappy to leave Carol's place. Even though I adored her family, I felt uncomfortable, as if I were sabotaging their family unit. That concern lived inside me, not them. I felt I didn't fit in there or anywhere. I was grateful to my "foster" family, but ashamed that my own family was not loving.

Unsent Letter

Dear Me,

I think I'm beginning to love you.

Carry the lessons of love

from Carol's family.

-32-
The University of Poison

We drove to a house I had never visited before, without much conversation. Nothing was said about the drug accusation or the command to get out of her house and not come back. It was as if it had never happened. Nothing unusual. Just the same family stuff. All pushed aside. Pretending again.

Turning off the highway, my mother stopped in a clean, white driveway. Her friend's new house sat on a blue-water canal in a spacious estate, with many bedrooms and a long white couch. I remember thinking it was so soft and comfortable.

My mother and Anna had been friends for many years. Anna's husband worked away for half the year, then returned for six months. With free time, Anna made new friends, despite raising her family.

Anna's family had moved from inner Brisbane to the canal house about twelve months earlier. Visiting her and her family felt safe, surrounded by kind and familiar people. The new home felt like a display home, with all-new furniture. I could smell it as I first walked inside. It was orderly, tidy, and squeaky clean.

Inside and outside the house, I couldn't help but envy
Anna and her boys. They had all new belongings and,
best of all, they lived on a blue water estate. Their dad
even called home every week. I wanted a family like that.

A daydreamy family with both a mother and father who
cared, all living together, where people have their own
stuff. A place to call home where everyone belonged!

They were so lucky!

The morning after we arrived at Anna's, my mother left. I
was never told where or why.

I stayed with Anna for three long months. My mother,
however, would return now and again, and the two
would combine their drinking marathons: beer, Scotch,
Champagne, and wine, both red and white! Whatever
alcohol was available would be poured down their
throats, glass after glass.

I did not experience much of my mother in her mothering
role when living at Anna's. She was emotionally distant,
especially when in drinking mode. And, as she was in her
drinking form whenever she visited, there was little to no
engagement with me, her daughter.

I could not process this new life in any depth, its
highlights and lowlights. I accepted I had a new fatherless
life and now an almost motherless life. I didn't work or
attend school for those three months. Unsurprising again.

Living with Anna and her family, I soon began to see
the loneliness in her kids' eyes, a look that mirrored my
own. At first, the new house and its sparkle made me feel
hopeful, safe even. As weeks went by, I realised the silence
covered their loneliness, too. Surrounded by new things
but without their father, they carried the same ache as

I did. I felt both connection and disappointment as my illusions faded.

The dream family I had revered at the beginning of my stay did not exist.

Unfortunately, my new home with Anna mirrored the life I thought I had left behind. Anna drank as often as my mother, matching her pace and volume. Their laughter quickly turned to misery as they drank for hours, sadness spilling out between sobs. I watched their conversations spiral from camaraderie to sorrow, the cycle of pain taking hold, confirming that the safety I felt was only fleeting.

Anna copied my mother's behaviour's, sometimes calling friends while drunk. Her late-night rants aired the miseries that wore down her will to live.

I knew this Theatre of Behaviours all too well; this was the prelude to the main act. The same daily sounds of 1-5-8. Zsstt. The stubby lid fizzed at the first touch before detaching, each stubby lid falling onto the kitchen table. The long breath out after a long swig in. The stubby landing noisily on the table. The stare into nothingness.

Alcohol numbed their steady, excruciating pain, just as students commit to long exam study sessions. Their resolve was firm.

The next day, as with so many others after their drinking marathons, I woke to the echoes of Anna's tears and drunken conversation. The kitchen table still bore the stains from the previous night. I learned to move quietly among the family, feigning calm and mimicking their rhythms so chaos wouldn't spill onto Anna's kids or me. I felt trapped; life again meant hiding my true feelings beneath layers of performance, both noisy and silent at once.

Their combined drinking sessions were all the same yet different too:

Drinking alcohol to stop the misery, drinking

drink after drink, drinking

drink to forget, drinking

slurring speech, drinking

crying, drinking,

wet mascara running down the face, drinking.

Unable to stand up after drinking.

No dinner is prepared again, drinking.

Unable to lift their heads from drinking.

Blind-eyed drinking.

Soul-crushing, life-destroying drinking.

Anna and my mother together championed each of those types of drinking sessions.

For me, it was all frightening: the lead-up, the event itself, the aftermath, and the recovery. Worst of all, I hated pretending the next day, the acting, make-believing life was good.

The shame I witnessed in the pretence of a forced smile, the lowering of a gaze away from mine, and their body's slow movements taught me that this was how one lived in a body slowly combusting under the weight of shame.

I drew on my own survival methods during those times, recalling breathing strategies and public presentation techniques I had practiced hundreds of times before.

Pretending. Acting.

As the entertainer I once was, I mimicked Anna's secret remorse just as I had mimicked my mother's. I pretended everything was fine, playing the "smiley-faced, happy girl" and ignoring the last night's sadness.

Unfortunately, at Anna's, I came to understand more deeply that pretending only masked my pain. The strategy I used, smiling and acting happy, brought me no inner relief. My suffering remained, though fooling others became easier. I felt the gap between my cheerful exterior and the truth beneath grow wider, making my daily actions increasingly hollow.

I pretended so well that everyone thought I was happy.

And that was my goal.

-33-
Regular Irregularities

I suffered because of my mother's behaviour and had to raise myself. I also analysed my own alarming behaviours. Not being able to speak up and tell the truth became my life's work. When my mother returned to the Gold Coast from Brisbane for good, it signalled a new chapter for us. We left Anna's and moved into our own rental.

The small, bright unit had two bedrooms, a laundry, a bathroom, a lounge, and a kitchen. It felt warm and homely. I loved it.

I didn't return to work. Instead, I enrolled in the local high school to finish my secondary education. I felt embarrassed attending the initial interview after missing months of school. I was used to feeling small when it came to my education. I knew I wouldn't be taken seriously by the counsellor at my enrolment interview. I hadn't been taken seriously before because of my frequent school absences.

At the interview, my mother and I sat quietly as the guidance counsellor read the previous school reports. His eyebrows rose, signalling questions. Nothing about this gave me confidence.

I wondered what was written in that report. No one at my previous school had asked why I hadn't attended regularly. My parents had never mentioned whether the school had called to ask about my absences. I never did homework or completed assignments. My marks were appalling. Even without reading the report card, I guessed it said something like: this student requires as much assistance as possible, as she is not attending school regularly enough to be reported upon.

Best of luck, you poor bastards.

The guidance counsellor finally asked why I wanted to return to school. I told him, despite my shame and humiliation, that I dreamed of being a teacher and inspiring kids to learn. He looked into my eyes, then at my mother.

"Based on all the accounts in this report card, your daughter doesn't have the attendance record to be reported on in the first place. She also doesn't seem to have the aptitude or academic qualifications required to become a teacher. She wouldn't be able to get into college to become a teacher."

Sigh!

After the interview, I was asked to leave while my mother and the counsellor talked. About ten minutes later, my mother returned. She said I would start school the following Monday. I asked what was discussed, and my mother said, "Not a lot."

And that was that.

I started school on Monday, feeling extremely nervous. In my new uniform, I stood out like a fireworks display. My latest black lace-up leather shoes were especially noticeable. I was probably one of only twenty kids in the whole beachside school wearing regular school shoes. Most wore white thongs or sandshoes without socks. I was identified as a "Briso" almost immediately. Making friends with the locals wasn't easy.

Nothing changed as weeks turned into months. I felt different from the other students. I was shy and awkward, and I lacked confidence, which made me ashamed of my life. I wasn't dressed like the others. I wore the full uniform as required, probably the only student to do so. Many of the senior students looked so cool, wearing white thongs, light blue jumpers, sun-bleached hair, and carefree attitudes. I wore fear and insecurity. They knew it, and I eventually learned it, too.

Sadly, though, I didn't know it at the time.

By the September holidays, I knew my mother was worried about finances again. I heard her talk about it endlessly. I decided to leave school again because it was a "sometimes place" for me. It was almost impossible to stay in school, so I went looking for a job. I needed to help the family move out of borderline poverty and uncertainty and into a better financial life.

I wish the school counsellor who had told my mother that I wouldn't be able to become a teacher because I didn't have the capacity in me to learn had spoken with me before I decided to leave school again. I regretted that decision eventually.

I applied for several jobs and got one almost immediately. I worked for an insurance company as a Customer Service Officer. I quickly learned the processes and thoroughly enjoyed my semi-autonomous role. I transitioned into administrative roles, abandoning my aspiration to become a teacher.

My favourite part of this story is that the guidance officer didn't know what he was talking about, given that I since spent thirty years in classrooms. I taught beautiful children in a teacher support role, sharing some of the most amazing things with them. In turn, they taught me some of life's best lessons.

Teaching hundreds of children across prep, primary, and secondary schools in my support role is one of my most outstanding achievements to date.

-34-
A Day Off

Amidst the early days spent on the beach, amidst the tears and uncertainty of leaving our father and our house, I was still in a state of confusion. I had always wanted to live apart from my father, but reality was different from what I expected.

My mind was overwhelmed as I tried to take charge of my life and figure out what it should look like within my smaller family. It was all-consuming. I could not compartmentalise any of it; contemplation was tricky as I couldn't think constructively, only simply. Sometimes I didn't know I could feel. The whole of me was numb some days.

The weekend before starting my new job in the insurance office, I recall sitting on the beautiful sandy beach near our new unit, feeling a mix of overwhelm and confusion, yet also the happiness of moving to a unit all our own. Finally, we were moving away from our past misery and unhappy memories and onto a new life, in new surroundings at this sunny, sandy, surf beach.

I felt blessed to be where I was on that day.

Creeping into the exquisite vision of sun, surf, and beach were memories from the day in Brisbane city, a day that significantly changed my life. It was a day that took so much more from me than I could have ever predicted or imagined.

We were living at the time in a small, dark, cold little unit in Brisbane, and since moving there, my mother had been drinking more heavily than usual. I'd just had my fourteenth birthday, so I was still living with my mother.

Three months into a new job, my mother's smile each day told me she was not as depressed as she had been; her demeanour was happy, and her energy was high, albeit she was drinking more heavily.

I was glad to see her so happy so often. My mother earned a regular income, and now that we lived in one home without having to leave at a moment's notice, my world and hers had become more stable.

I had visited her workplace recently on a couple of afternoons after school for an hour or so, and she had made me the most delicious pizza for afternoon tea and poured me my favourite sarsaparilla soft drink in a tall glass.

I'd said a quick hello to her new boss and had a brief look around the gorgeous old hotel building and the huge beer garden where my mother's little lunch bar was situated. My mother really liked not just the work environment, but also her boss, Mrs. Vivienne Carlisle. They became good friends.

Mrs. Vivienne Carlisle looked like a movie star to me. Her elegance and poise stood out in the crowd. Her blonde hair was perfectly styled, and she wore clothes which I had never seen in real life, diamonds on her fingers, gold chains hanging from her neck. Vivienne's makeup was aglow, subtle, and beautifully matched to her skin.

About four months into my mother's new job, she told me not to get dressed for school because I was going to work with her.

She wanted to show me exactly what she did and promised me another good look around the hotel. She was excited for us both to visit her workplace for the day. I was to "dress nicely" because I was going to meet some of her new work friends. I thought this was a little strange, but I did exactly what I was told, as I had always been trained to do. My obedience was ingrained.

It was 10am on the dot when we arrived in the beer garden, and I helped my mother organise her workstation - food, and more food, for the hundreds of pizza and toasted sandwich orders she would receive. Not too long into sandwich-making, I was introduced to some of her new coworkers, who were also busy setting tables and chairs and opening giant umbrellas, making the beer garden look like a relaxing outdoor eatery.

A young man named Kelvin came by, and my mother introduced us. Kelvin looked about twenty, clean-shaven, and nice enough, and he offered to buy me a sarsaparilla from the inside bar. I love sarsaparilla! We were sitting and chatting near my mother's workstation when the boss came over to say a few words. It looked to me like she knew Kelvin. We continued talking, and then my mother quietly let me know that, since she would be working, I'd be spending a couple of hours with Kelvin.

Together, we walked through the hotel as he showed me the beautiful refurbishments. It was exciting to be personally escorted around the lovely old hotel instead of being at school. After a good look through the bars and beer garden, Kelvin led me up a very narrow staircase to the top floor.

Walking along the corridor, I realised just how many rooms there were for overnight stays. I was shocked to learn that people stayed overnight at hotels. I thought people typically booked into resort-type places for a holiday stay, rather than hotels.

Kelvin stopped somewhere near the end of the long corridor and took a key from his pocket. He opened the door, and I followed him inside. Immediately, I noticed the room was orderly, clean, and neat. I could stay here overnight if I ever needed a place to sleep. I was still in exploring mode and appreciated Kelvin showing me so much of the hotel, including the rooms. I thought maybe we were there to watch TV for a while. But then, there wasn't a TV!

Kelvin turned back to close the door behind him, then came towards me and wrapped his arms around my waist. I took a step back, and Kelvin took two steps forward, and there we were, locked together. Kelvin walked me backwards to the bed and attempted to push me down. It all happened in a moment, and I became frightened. I didn't understand, so I began to sit up, but Kelvin gently pushed me back down again. He lay close beside me for a moment, then began undoing his belt. He started unzipping his jeans, and by the time he pulled himself out of his jeans, he had made a sticky mess on himself and me. Of course, I was unaware of what had happened until it had happened, but now I guessed!

Did Kelvin think he was going to have sex with me? I felt uncomfortable and embarrassed, scared and confused, so I tried to sit up again. "Get off me, Kelvin," I said in a voice that made it clear I was not impressed and shocked, perhaps!

Kelvin was busy with his sticky mess and, pointing to his unzipped jeans, told me that I was to make him "erect" again. "Get me hard, will ya?"

He took hold of himself, took my hand, and together we tried to make him erect again.

His legs were over mine, so I couldn't easily move. My head and my insides were full of nerves. Did my mother know I was up here in this room?

What would she think if she knew what I was being forced to do?

She was downstairs working, and I was up here doing something I shouldn't be doing and didn't want to do with this boy I didn't even know.

I could be in trouble because this was her workplace and....

Hell, I hope he's locked that door. No, I hope he hasn't. I hope he's left it open because maybe I can get out and back downstairs!

But I can't get up, so I hope he's locked it. I hoped no one came in that door, ssw us, and then went downstairs to tell my mother!

My mind was going in circles. I was in full panic mode. Please help me, somebody!

I wanted to scream out to her, to tell her what was happening, because if I told her later and wasn't believed, she could lose her job, and I could be in trouble, and my mother could be in trouble, too! I couldn't be the reason she lost the new job she loved so much.

But it was not my fault; I didn't ask for this to happen!
I don't know how to do what I'm supposed to be doing,
and he's angrily telling me, "Hurry up, let's get this thing
happenin'. You know we're havin' sex. Come on, don't
you wanna have sex with me? I saw you here last week
when you came in to see your mother, and I really wanna
have sex with you."

I didn't know where to look or what to say. Kelvin
pushed against my chest. I held myself stiffly, but he
pushed harder. I stared at the wall. "Do exactly what
you're told; be safe," I told myself. I lay completely
flat, and Kelvin lay on top of me, but I kept my legs
together. I was so scared, shaking, frightened by what was
happening.

I didn't want to have sex with Kelvin, but I did, because
he told me I was going to, and he was forcing himself
onto me. I was too scared to yell out, too frightened not
to let him do what he wanted, and too frightened to
breathe.

I closed my eyes and turned my head away as Kelvin
pushed, snorting, telling me how long he'd been waiting
to have sex with the daughter of the new worker at the
beer garden bar.

I wanted to pull his hair, scratch his eyes out, and strike
him. But I didn't. I was sweating with fear; he was
sweating profusely.

Tilting his body forward once again, Kelvin finally fell
onto my chest and stayed there, sweat running from his
forehead, panting like a dog needing water. I hated every
bead of his wet sweat that dripped onto me.

I did not want to feel like this again. I was so ashamed
that I hardly tried to run away, and I just accepted what

was happening. Why didn't I fight him more? Why didn't I push him away harder? He was just like that disgusting, grunting, sweating Tim from our holiday, taking from young women and from me! Is this what I was meant to do? Lie there, take orders, and listen to men tell me what they wanted? It made me so angry to be the vessel for men's sex acts. Is that what sex was? I didn't want it to be like that. I wanted to scream and cry out loud! Get Off Me!

I wanted to tell my father and wanted him to come here and, because of Kelvin, do precisely what he did to my mother, execute a perfectly landed backhand! But he wouldn't. I wouldn't even tell him. I'd tried to tell my father things, but it got me into trouble. I got my family into a big fight when I told on Tim. So, what did I do? I stayed quiet because it was easier to be silent. It kept everybody happy.

Did other girls my age have to do these things? Did other girls my age have men crawl over them? If they did, did they want to scream and hit out at them? If I had my softball bat, I would have smacked him across the head with it.

I pushed and shoved at Kelvin in disgust, and he rolled off me.

Kelvin slowly got to his feet, pulled up his jeans, tidied himself, and walked to the door. Before he left, he turned back to look at me. I felt humiliated. I felt sick and wanted to cry. I needed to scream, to yell to my mother, "This is what's happened, again, and I'm a part of it. I want it all to stop."

I really wanted to tell my father, but I knew I wouldn't. I couldn't face another one of his scoldings. Kelvin turned towards the door and left without a word.

I sat up, crying out loudly. I didn't know where to begin my next move. I tidied my hair with my fingers, wiped my tears, and stared at the confused, humiliated face I saw in the mirror.

I slumped back onto the bed, still crying. I wanted to go downstairs, but I couldn't yet. I couldn't pull myself together enough to stop crying. I stayed there on the bed, thinking about Kelvin and what I would tell my mother.

What would I tell her? The truth? Would she believe me? I was unsure.

I again rubbed my tears away. Looking in the small mirror, I saw an honest face. My mother should believe me. I was her daughter!

Slowly, I found the courage to decide return downstairs. It had been a while since Kelvin left.

"Hello."

Unsent Letter

SCREAM!

-35-
It's Robert

"Hi," said a deep voice, "it's Robert!"

Robert? Who was Robert? I looked up, scared, wondering who this man was and what he was doing in this room. Robert moved slowly, then gently closed the door and walked towards me, just like Kelvin. He wrapped me in his arms and tried to kiss me. I pulled my head away from Robert.

My guess is he was about thirty to forty years old.

Robert held my head, cradling it in his hand like a baby, and kissed my head as he ran his hands through my hair. I was at a loss, scared, on edge. Robert began telling me the same things Kelvin had: how he'd seen me with my mother in my school uniform and how he'd been thinking about me, pressing his mouth to mine with urgency. The urgency of the kiss stunned me. The force! Debilitating!

I don't have to write the rest, do I? You can imagine what Robert was thinking about: a teenage girl in a school uniform, living out the much-desired fantasy in his mind.

I pushed Robert away, albeit gently. I was in mental hell. Robert gently pulled my head to his chest, kissing my hair.

How did he know where I was? It felt like he knew where to find me and knew me, too!

"We'll be fine, darling. I'll be gentle, sweetheart; you'll be okay."

I took a huge breath, screaming inside, beaten again, burying my head further into his chest, where I stayed, trying to comfort myself.

My stomach churned, a little less than before, but my breathing was stilted while Robert walked me backwards, just like Kelvin, and laid me on the messed-up bed.

I watched Robert take off his blue suit jacket, telling me how beautiful this moment would be.

Should I have known he was coming to see me?

Well, I didn't.

I felt nervous. Tears welled up in my eyes. I felt alone and afraid. This couldn't be happening!

I wondered in that moment if my mother knew where I was. Come upstairs, please, Mum, come looking for me!

Had my mother seen Kelvin, and did she ask where I was? Maybe she was going to come upstairs soon.

Robert was lying on top of me, and maybe she wouldn't blame me if she saw it. After all, Sam used to climb all over her, and she didn't like it, so maybe she'd believe I didn't want or like what was happening to me either.

Robert took a very long time to squirm and wriggle on me. The crisp collar of his white shirt pushed into my face as he lurched higher. Both hurt a lot.

My anguish, my impatience, and humiliation were growing into anger like a dancing flame inside me. It felt like my body could ignite as I lay silently under another man taking from me, quietly imploring him to burn from the inside out.

The act of sex, the pushing, hurt so much. All I wanted was for it to stop. He kept talking to himself about sex as the angst in me became a stinging sensation. At that point, I needed to hold my arms still. I was frightened I was going to grab his hair and pull it out or hit him on the back… His breath became louder, and then… Robert finally stopped.

I felt the warmth inside me. His body eventually fell limp on mine. I lay still, my intolerance building in my head! Robert rolled off me and lay as if sunbaking, with a smile and a glow about him, saying how wonderful that moment had been for him and how fantastic it was to make love to such a young girl.

I wanted to stab him.

He finally stood up. I lay on my side, pulled my knees up, and covered myself with my dress. A replay of a similar act played out just before Robert arrived. I lay there till Robert was ready to leave. He put on his suit coat, kissed me on the head, and thanked me for some beautiful moments that he would never forget.

I had no words. I didn't understand. I said nothing because I didn't know what to say. What words could I have spoken to a man three times my age, indulging in a fantasy about me, a schoolgirl who was to lie still for a man and be mute because I was his desire? Couldn't these men who wanted lots of sex buy a blow-up doll or pay a prostitute and live out their fantasies that way?

I wasn't worrying about my mother anymore, because I couldn't fit another worry into my brain. I didn't care whether she was looking for me, what Kelvin had told her, how he had a key to the room, how Robert knew I was upstairs, or whether my mother's boss knew I was upstairs. My mind was numb.

When I could, I got up and closed the door. I wasn't opening it for anyone.

I straightened myself up once again. I washed my face until the tears stopped. I tried to clean the men's sticky mess off my blue dress, trying not to make it look too obvious, and sat on the bed again for ages.

Then, slowly and ashamedly, I walked back down the hallway, down the stairs, through the hotel, and out to the beer garden to the kitchen to face my mother. To my gut-wrenching surprise, both Kelvin and Robert were seated not far from the kitchen, having lunch together.

I saw my mother and couldn't help but wonder if she wore the biggest smile in the beer garden. There was something about my mother's smile; when she smiled, she lit up a room. I wasn't mistaking this smile; it was extra beautiful. My mother didn't ask me anything: not where I'd been, nor what I had been doing, nor even why Kelvin had come back to the beer garden before me. I didn't want her to know why my blue dress was wet in places. My entire being, my mind and body, went numb again.

My mother offered me lunch, but I couldn't eat anything. I bought another sarsaparilla and sat just outside the kitchen, wondering what I was really doing at her workplace. How did I get myself into these situations? What could I do to avoid them? How could I start screaming in these situations? How could I convince my parents to believe me when I told them what was happening to me in these situations?

I didn't want to allow it. I didn't want to have sex; it was uncomfortable, stinging, horrible sex that those men took. Was that what men wanted women for, so they could get something from them, and was the thing they wanted so badly what we had? Was that what love was? Was love the thing girls had that men wanted? Was that love, or just sex? My mother told me I was only to have sex when I was married. Sex was for a time when you loved someone.

Was that what just happened to me, the loving sex women must have with men? Or was this the random sex girls talked about at school? Either way, I didn't want it. I wasn't doing it. I couldn't be the only girl in the world who didn't like what just happened, surely? There had to be other things to do when you were in love, nicer things than that sex. Those questions filled my head.

I didn't look at Kelvin or Robert, but my mother talked to them, and her boss talked to them, and they were all smiling; all of them except me.

I felt like a used vessel, something to fill up to get what they wanted before pulling out and walking away. It didn't make any sense to me. If this was what the big, exciting thing called sex was about, it was not for me.

No, my mother would never put me in that situation. She wouldn't, so who sent the men? Why did they send the men?

Robert knew Kelvin and knew where we were. He knew he was going to have sex! He did. He said, "It will be okay, darling," or something like that. He knew. Did Kelvin tell him? He must have. Why was Kelvin doing this to me? If my mother knew, she would be so angry. I hoped she would be, anyway.

My mother didn't ask me about my day, and I didn't tell her. Nothing was said on the way home in the car. Arriving at our house, I showered straightaway, rubbing my skin clean of Kelvin and Robert's memory again, scrubbing the essence of their bodies from mine, yet all the rubbing and cleansing failed to erase the dirty, shameful feelings inside me. It was impossible.

I lived with the debilitating shame and unknowing of how sex with unknown men was happening in my life.

Unsent Letter

Dear Little One

This is a new and bloody frightening phase of life.

Stay upright, stay aware, stay safe.

No matter what.

-36-

Another Again

It was late Saturday morning, and I was basking in the sun shining through our loungeroom window in our little beachside unit. Someone knocked on our front door. My mother met the visitor and immediately invited him inside.

She gestured Greg towards the kitchen table, where they sat talking for a long time.

Greg was a young guy who looked about twenty, with unkempt, longish, sun-bleached hair. He looked like a surfer, wearing faded olive green boardshorts that reached his knees, a large rip at the shoulder of his cream t-shirt, and a grubby, out-of-shape, sloppy joe tied around his shoulders. He wore nothing on his feet.

It took me a few quick, sneaky looks at his face before I recognised him as a guy who went to one of my high schools. He acted a little odd, from what I remember, the most bizarre kind of cool.

What the hell was HE doing here, I wondered.

And why was my mother talking to him? Upon looking, he reminded me of the year twelve bloke who used to brag about taking drugs. The one who was popular with the cool girls because he looked like a sun-kissed surfer boy who took drugs. And that was definitely something high school girls found cool.

He looked at least three to four years older than me.

I wondered how my mother knew someone who reminded me of a boy I didn't know from high school. I didn't know. Maybe he was the stalker who had sent me an unsigned letter a few months before? Wanting to meet me!

Looking closer at him, on my way past the kitchen table to my bedroom, I noticed his eyes were bloodshot.

I went to my bedroom to get him out of my line of sight.

It was after midday when my mother came into my bedroom. "Throw a few things in a bag. You're going away for the night."

I look up at her, wincing!

"Yes, you are," she sang, nodding her head. "You're going now. Hurry up."

With the rolling of my eyes and one deep breath, I followed her directions as always.

Unhappily. As always.

I embodied that ritual as my norm.

Leaving my home to go somewhere with Greg didn't feel okay. It felt just like when my parents sent me away to the Gold Coast with people I did not know. They sent me away so often, and now it was happening once again.

I hated this midday now, more than any other recent midday.

With my bag packed, I put on my thongs and walked out the door.

Peeved.

The car waiting for me was an old, small, and rusty model. The light green vehicle rattled and made loud noises when Greg started it.

And off we went, without question, to an unknown destination with my smiley mother waving us off.

We rattled along the streets of suburbia until we reached the green hills of the hinterland. I sat as close as I could to the passenger door, putting as much space between Greg and me as possible. The car moved slowly and steadily for about two long hours before it made its way up a long, steep hill.

Finally, at the summit, the bitumen road stopped, and the new gravel road crunched under the wheels. The yellowish gravel crackled and popped, producing heavy dust.

Nothing had changed in my demeanour in the hours since leaving home. I still didn't want to be in this car with this druggo I didn't know. I really wanted to be in my living room, where I belonged. And if this car kept struggling and broke down, I would be happy to get out, run to a phone booth, and call my mother to get me, even though I wouldn't be able to tell her where I was.

But I didn't have money with me to make that telephone call, if there was a telephone box in this hinterland. And anyway, we didn't have a home phone.

I conceded I felt scared and lost.

Thank goodness the car suddenly stopped and parked beside a small grey shed. The same kind of shed I'd seen in my 1-5-8 neighbourhood. Jumping out of the car, I stretched my body, my arms, and especially my legs while looking across acres of farmland.

And Greg drove away.

 Staring at the car in motion, I froze.

Then, I began walking back down the gravel road to the bitumen. My breath was heavy as I stood at the side of the road, wanting to run. But I didn't. I stood immobile, my mind racing while wishing for a car to appear so I could get help to get me home to safety.

Not one random car appeared.

But Greg's car did.

His car drove back on the gravel driveway, with the same dust in the air and the same crushing, crackling sounds from the car wheels.

From the driver's seat, he pointed to the shed. I turned to follow his instructions. By the time I reached the parked car, Greg was opening the shed door, gesturing for me to get inside. I immediately smelled something stale, like water that had lain dormant for a long time. I couldn't miss the dust particles in the air as they were thick and cloying; net-like cobwebs floated above me.

There was no flooring, just dirt. In the far corner of the shed, I noticed a wet spot on the muddy ground, which smelled really bad.

Against the shed wall was a dusty table on a lean and two wooden chairs. The chairs were not under the table, as they would be if someone was taking care of the inside of this shed, but positioned on their own, away from the table. On the table was a small bag of green beans. Not falling or rolling off, but stable on the table, albeit it was on a lean.

Greg pointed out that the beans were our dinner that evening.

I didn't want his beans; they were probably part of his drugs, owned by a cartel.

What if he was in a cartel? I was scared that they might all turn up.

What does this night away from home really mean, Greg? I suddenly thought.

As darkness fell, Greg lit a candle. One candle rested with the green bean drugs on the table.

There had been little conversation as I was uninterested in the goings on in the shed. Anger at both Greg and my mother was my secondary state of mind, as the sick feeling in my stomach wouldn't go away. Greg sat on the other chair, opened the bean bag, and offered it to me. I was hungry enough to take a few. I had decided to eat the green beans after all. Seated on a chair, munching on a bean, Greg pulled something else from a plastic bag from his pocket, also green.

He rolled it in three white cigarette papers, lit it, and took a long, intense breath in. He offered me some of the long cigarettes, as a ring of smoke he made with his mouth filled the air. But I shook my head, no.

What I wanted was to be home in my warm pyjamas, sipping homemade soup, sitting on the lounge in front of the heater. Instead, my mother fed her usual desire to be alone by ridding herself of her daughter, so she farmed me out again. This time to a farm.

I bet her last night away wasn't spent in the middle of who knows where, with someone she didn't know or trust smoking long green cigarettes that didn't look or smell like ordinary cigarettes. Nor, I suspected, would she be inclined to eat an offering of suspect green beans for dinner.

Remember, I've been in this play before. Not the same, but similar.

Unknown men equals five.

The purpose of being with this unknown man right now?

Scared to be alone with this unknown man: one hundred percent.

Results of this night away: not in yet.

I felt trapped, like I was in a kidnapping movie. No one knew where I was except the kidnapper. The main difference between the movie and my experience was that people in the movie were always searching for the kid.

The night air grew cooler. I was shaking from the cold, wearing a short-sleeve T-shirt, track pants, and thongs.

Greg finished drawing on his long, green-filled cigarette and threw the end bit into the muddy patch near the corner of the shed. He threw a few thin, dirty, dusty blankets on the floor. Dust filled the cold air as they hit the dirt floor. I quickly fashioned one blanket under me and lay down, then pulled the other one over me. Still, it was bitterly cold.

Before Greg fashioned his makeshift bed for the evening, he blew out the candle! The one small candle. The atmosphere in the shed grew even eerier in the darkness.

I rolled myself into a ball to keep warm. As I lay on the dusty floor with the old dusty blankets on top of me, I hoped Greg would lie as far from me as possible, but he didn't. He lay down beside me, his body touching mine. It felt warmer with a body close to mine in this cold shed, but I would rather have lain alone and frozen to death.

I could feel Greg's body stirring and fidgeting next to me, edging closer. Then, he wrapped his arms around me.

I edged away, and he edged towards me. Then the rubbing! His body was rubbing up against my backside.

Trying to keep warm, was he? I pretended this could be true.

The rubbing transitioned into a push, then another, a thrust into my body.

Greg continued to grind against me, then a purposeful heave pushed my body away from his. I didn't react in that moment. Not once.

Lying on the rough, dusty, uneven dirt floor was hideously uncomfortable, making it more difficult to move and escape him and his agenda.

-37-

The Surge

Having to contend with the man behind, grinding his body into mine, was difficult to ignore, but I chose not to react.

Inside, my stomach felt like a hamster running on its wheel, racing, spinning 'til I was nauseated.

Did I run? To where? Where was I? I didn't know.

My eyes whizzed around the shed, trying to think straight to stop the hamster on the wheel inside me. I inhaled, held it, then slowly let it out.

It was in letting my breath out slowly that I decided not to run.

I could feel him against my thighs. He grabbed at my arm, pulling my clothing, tugging at it and me until I twisted onto my back.

His nude body edged slowly and gauchely onto mine. He continued to grind his flesh against what was left of my clothing. His weight on mine was painful, given the hard earth underneath us, and I screamed out in irritation and angst as I pushed him hard. Rolling off me, he lay still. I lay silent. I tried to hold my breath and temper but lost both. I was afraid now, afraid of what might happen if I hit out in frustration. I'd acted out in a situation like this before, copping a smack across the face and a threat of strangulation. My breath was growing increasingly rapid and loud, then, almost breathless.

His rough, cold hand rested on my arm for a moment, then tugged hard and suddenly, pulling the blanket from me. I grabbed it, trying to rip it from his hands, but he held tight. This time, he tugged firmly at my clothing with both hands. He moved towards me, trying to straddle my body.

It was going to happen! My breath stilled!

He struggled to anchor his body upon mine. I assumed the drug cigarette had taken effect, and I waited, hoping, wishing for him to fall limp.

He didn't. There was the grunting. Then repeated heaving and lurching. Then it all stopped before it began again. The pain in my back and legs was immense as he threw himself into me, forcing my body into the hard earth. My inner flame from the entire madness was incalculable.

Done, his body fell onto mine. He lay there for a short while.

Relieved and disgusted at him, I pushed him off me, and he let me. I rolled away, but he edged towards me. There we were next to each other again.

I was appalled at him for forcing himself on me. I was shocked at myself for not fighting harder, for not fighting him off.

I wanted to fight and did, but it wasn't enough. I was too stunned, too alone, too hellishly scared to fight hard.

I knew fighting unknown men who wanted sex was dangerous; my mother had done it with my father and lost. I had done it before this night too. I did it and lost, which left me completely confused, especially when I was underneath him, fighting him, a man who wanted my body.

I eventually drift away from the experience of the horrors in this shed. Away to the beach and the safety of Billy, Mark, and my friends.

I went numb.

I felt nothing.

As I returned to my body, I felt, once again, the aftermath of the clumsy, forceful body that wanted more from me.

After he returned to my body, I felt disgust, then nothing.

He had infuriated me before; now I felt more than that, and nothing else. I was regularly woken through the night by the weight of his clumsy body pressing on me, his disregard for me, and my fighting against him.

The fact that I eventually gave in sickened me.

I paid the price to stay safe.

Pay the price to be safe. Pay the price to be safe. It's time to be still, don't move!

I lay stiff.

More nausea followed, more profound disgrace at myself, a truly grief-filled body of shame and sleeplessness.

Another sordid, sickening act that I could not control alone. One more dent in my tiny soul!

I watched the moon through the side window before falling asleep. Greg was snoring loudly by now.

Thank goodness.

Waking before Greg as the sun rose, I quietly wrapped myself in the dusty, dirty blankets and stood near the shed door. The farm shed was freezing, even colder than the night before. Not too long after Greg opened his eyes, I told him I wanted to go home.

I must have sounded deadly serious because he got up, dressed, and went to the car.

We drove down the gravel road leading onto the long, steep hill and took the long drive through the rural hills back into suburbia.

Neither of us said a single word.

Greg dropped me off at home and took off immediately.

My mother wasn't at home when I arrived, but I wished like hell she had been home. I really wanted her to be home.

I jumped into a long, hot shower to wash dirt and dust and worst of all, him from me, the nauseating concentrate of his essence, loathsome man. I scrubbed him from my body!

As I stood under the warm shower, my mind kept firing questions. How did my mother know Greg? How did he know where I lived? Did she know I didn't know him? How could she have trusted him with her daughter? Did she know where she sent her daughter overnight? Did she know what he wanted from her daughter during the overnight stay?

I wanted so badly to tell her what he wanted from me. But I didn't.

The more often men took from me, the more paralysed I became and the less I could use my voice.

I told no one, and no one asked me about my overnight stay.

If my mother knew what I did to keep safe, would she understand? The same questions looped round my tired, drained mind.

Did she? Did she know? She didn't, I bet. The questions continued to crowd me.

It was easier to stay safe before I was underneath a man, but once I was, I was trapped, with nowhere to go and no one to rescue me.

I eventually gave in, Mother! That's what I did to stay safe. Help me, please!

Then I kept it all secret, another act in the ongoing play I lived.

My mother arrived home around 6pm that evening.

Zsstt...

Zsstt...

Zsstt...

Before I talked to her, I tried to read her face, staring at her to find...something. I didn't know exactly what it would look like, but I was looking for something that told me she cared where her daughter had been, where she had been taken, what she had done, and what he had done.

Some look of care and consideration, that said, "I'm here for you. Tell me everything."

I saw nothing.

Heard only Zsstt...

Was there something missing in her?

To spend time childless, she would risk sending her daughter with anyone, anywhere.

Yes, that was the answer to my question.

She wanted to be alone, kid-less. Get on with her life of drinking alone, in the dark, and staring out the door, at the blank wall or the ground.

As hard as I tried and as much as I wanted, I could not ask my mother anything, not one thing, about Greg.

I wanted to speak up because I felt like I was being taken advantage of by men I didn't know. But why?

My parents took advantage of my body by trying to break my bones, tearing my skin, and obstructing my breath until I blacked out. Grooming me and gaslighting me.

Drunk, stinking older adults took advantage of my body.

So-called girlfriends' boyfriends took advantage of it.

And the boys took advantage of it.

Exhausted and still nauseous, my mind continued to loop.
I had no thoughts beyond survival when I was with Greg.

Unsent Letter

My body has become others to use;

I am a servant to their own wants

Their actions make that clear.

My mind doesn't rest.

-38-
The Aftermath

I returned home from those debilitating hours completely spent. My body ached, my stomach churned, and every nerve felt raw from this man and all the men before him.

I felt sick, truly sick, not just from what had happened, but from the weight of shame that had settled deep inside me.

I didn't fully understand why I had been sent away that way. I kept thinking maybe my mother just wanted to be alone, as she often did. I didn't know, couldn't say, that there was any other reason. I felt trapped in my own confusion, carrying what had happened inside me, unable to share it with anyone.

Time passed, but my body did not forget.

Ten weeks later, I discovered I was pregnant.

I didn't tell my mother. Instead, I told one person I trusted completely, someone who could hold my pain with me without asking intrusive questions, silently and gently. Through them, I was introduced to a doctor who would speak with me. That was all I could manage.

I was terrified, ashamed, and exhausted. The world around me blurred; everything inside me felt like it was spinning, and yet I had to hold it all together.

Slamming Hughes

As a brand-new working girl, I had just found financial freedom that helped support both my mother and me. My life was kind of fun: sand, surf, freedom, a car, new colleagues at work, and nights out. Life felt better than ever, better than I had imagined.

Late one afternoon, dressed in her usual 5pm uniform of dressing gown and slippers, my mother said to me, 'Get dressed, dinner out tonight.'

Us? I wasn't sure what she meant, given that she was in her nightgown.

As usual.

I asked no questions and did as I was told, even though I now had new independence. Old behaviour patterns remained ingrained in me.

I showered and put on my lemon-coloured, swishy cotton dress, a summer dress with shoestring straps and frills around the neckline. It was a kind of maxi dress that showed off my suntan.

Wanting to show my mother my new dress, I looked for her in the bedroom and the lounge. Not finding her, I walked outside to the carport. There, I saw her standing on the footpath, chatting with a rather handsome thirty-something-year-old man I had recently met, a teacher from a high school I'd previously attended.

I stood by our car waiting for her when she called me over.

"Look who turned up here," she said with a smile.

"Good evening," he said, "don't you look lovely!"

"Thanks, Sir," I said without thinking!

I felt stupid. I wasn't a student anymore, so I didn't need to call him Sir. But what else did you call a teacher you only knew as Sir?

My mother then introduced me to him using his first name. "This is Hughes. He's just introduced himself to me. Do you remember him?"

Embarrassed? Absolutely! I smiled shyly and looked down. Oh God, how did he know where I lived?

"Well, if you're ready to go…," said Hughes to ME!

I think I raised my eyebrows. I'm not sure if he raised his.

I went back inside to grab my handbag, then I joined Hughes in his flashy little car and drove to our dinner. I wore my "what the hell" face, inside and out, though I was trying to remain calm. I tried not to seem rude or scared. This couldn't be happening. Another man wanting something from me? No way, not a chance.

We talked all the way to the quirky little restaurant and through dinner. I feared his agenda, yet I felt strong and in control. I'd been sent with men too many times before when it ended in nightmarish ways. This would not be one of those times.

The best part was that Hughes didn't touch me at all during dinner, nor did he try to put his arms around me or hold me. I felt okay so far.

As we left the restaurant, he took my hand as we walked to the car. It felt different, gentle, and I liked it a little. A soft kiss grew harder, more urgent for a moment. I gently turned my head and pulled away. I knew this kiss; knew it well. This one-act play I'd experienced many times before.

I can't say Hughes had the same agenda as the other men who had used and abused me in their one-act plays, yet Hughes' actions had potential.

Driving home, I sat as far from Hughes as possible, pressed against the far left of the seat, staring out of the window. I was silent and angry, and I'm sure it showed. That was my intention.

Outside my place, I opened the car door quickly. He grabbed my arm, pulling me closer.

"Aren't you going to give me a goodnight kiss?"

"No," I sang innocently! "Thank you for dinner, good night."

I slammed the door with attitude. I was angry, not just at Hughes. I was also angry at all the men who I could not stop from hurting and abusing me, yet I stopped HIM. The power of all of them, my whole abuse story, and my commitment to stop this abuse raged inside and outside me right then. It felt so powerful.

That slam said it all in one loud sound!

As I showered before bed, I had questions!

When was the dinner date with an ex-teacher arranged? And who had arranged it?

-40-
11.10pm

On a warm Saturday morning, I noticed the sunlight filtering through the tall trees. It was magical to see. Driving with my friend Carly through the rainforest reminded me of nature's beauty.

The radio played. We sang loudly and happily. That was our thing.

Singing out loud.

We were headed to the mountains to visit Carly's boyfriend, Daz. The quiet rainforest soon brought to us the most beautiful sounds of crickets, birds, and, oh, the scenery.

Arriving at Daz's, we changed into our togs and went straight to the creek, which ran by the bottom of his backyard. The sun was hot, the water calm and clear; the perfect way to spend the rest of Saturday.

After showering, we ate lunch while watching movies.

At dusk, we returned to the creek.

We were all a little sun-kissed, maybe too much. My skin was now red and stinging. Still, I loved the sun, so I wore my sunburn with joy.

So did Carly and Daz.

Dinner was easy, with a few beers and another movie.

Carly and Daz loved beer. I didn't drink it.

By the end of the movie, we were all plum tuckered. It was after 11pm.

As we got ready for bed, someone knocked. To our surprise, one of Daz's mates walked in Nate. The beers and conversation started again.

Who stops by at 11.10pm unannounced?

Exhausted, I couldn't really enjoy the friend's conversation.

-41-
The Fantasy

My bed for the night was the narrow vinyl couch in the lounge room, which was currently occupied by people! Finally, Daz called it a night, thank goodness, and Nate, his mate, got to his feet. Carly and Daz went to their bedroom as Nate walked to the front door.

"Shut the door after you," shouted Daz.

In the lounge, I laid the blanket on the couch, fluffed up the pillow, and fell into my bed.

"Lights out," called Daz.

"Goodnight, you two," I called.

A very short time later, as I lay on my bed, a sound came through the front doorway.

Nate walked back inside. Seating himself on the lounge, my bed for the evening, he bent towards me and whispered that he'd changed his mind, so was going to crash here the night.

Grabbing a blanket from a cupboard, he lay on the lounge room floor across from the narrow vinyl couch.

And me.

I didn't like this idea, his idea, at all. It felt Olympic champion-level discomfort to me.

And Nate did not stay on his own blanket across the room from me for long! He decided that the couch would be a better option.

Annoyingly, I found him sliding in beside me on the couch. With room for only one body, I told him to get back onto the floor, and back to the floor he went. This time, though, right beside the couch.

He arrived again, pushing his way onto the couch.

"Nate, get off the couch and leave me alone!" I stated angrily. He moved off the couch again to lie on the floor. Then he pulled at my blanket, so I climbed off the lounge to sleep on the floor, ripping my blanket from his grip.

"There, now I'm sleeping here," I pointed out, "and you can sleep there."

I rolled away from him so I couldn't see him. I hoped he got the message. Nate followed me to the floor! I whispered into his face, 'Leave me alone.'

He was growing stronger in his resolve to be close to me, and he remained deaf to my pleas. Not hearing that I didn't want him near me, he rolled himself onto me within the next minute. This time, he had hold of me. His strength, compared with mine, kept him in place. Was he more drunk than he had appeared earlier? Was he on weed? Where was the laughing, jovial, fun friend of Daz's now?

He'd disappeared.

I started to worry that he'd had more alcohol than the beers he'd drunk with my mates tonight. I was becoming even more concerned about his constant pushing and shoving toward me. I could not contain his strength. He told me to be quiet, the same way the men who had previously violated me had.

Be safe, don't be scared, I said to myself.

I wanted to call out to Carly; I really wanted her to come out to the lounge room to see what was happening.

But I didn't.

Again, I stayed quiet. Trained by experts.

As my frustrations grew, I became increasingly scared of him, especially when trying to fight him off. I gave up! He got exactly what he had come for.

He told me so.

To have sex with the girl from school he'd fantasised about.

Eventually, in the aftermath, he stood, pulled on his jeans, and left.

Disgusted with myself and him, knowing that I had given in to another contemptible man, knowing I'd let myself down, as I had promised myself I wouldn't, I eventually fell asleep.

I was angry at Nate.

I was consumed by anger toward myself for weeks on end. I couldn't get the push and shove out of my mind: the act and its aftermath.

I kept that night to myself for a long time. I asked my new doctor in recent times about the circumstances around that type of pressure to give your body over to a man for sex.

"It's called rape," he responded, "when you're pushing someone away, and you're saying no, go away, don't touch me, stop! Even if you're not screaming, and you're not physically lashing out for your life! If you're saying no in so many ways, and the man is ignoring you and continuing to push and shove their way onto and into your body, it's called rape."

It has taken me many years to bring my personal experiences of sexual abuse to the table and to be able to put them into words without my body filling with sorrowful emotions. Describing the feelings of fighting off the men who raped me, in different circumstances, and how those moments played out is nearly impossible for me.

It's all the same, though, no matter what the scenario is.

No consent = rape.

I lived with shame for many years, but I've since overcome it. Knowing I did all I could at the time to say no, making decisions in fear, and fighting until I had no fight left in me, has allowed me to see the truth of the situation.

I own my part in those frightful scenarios. Fear played a significant role in keeping me quiet, fighting silently but physically, and doing what was necessary to avoid being physically injured again. In situations that deny my voice, something happens to me that stops the scream from coming out, but the screaming continues inside long after the physical act is over.

That's what happened during the rapes I experienced. It's called going numb; it's a destabilising freeze. Fighting a drunk man who is grappling with your body in silence, in the dark, and in fear is debilitating, both emotionally and physically.

What does it feel like to be raped? In my case, whilst it was a physical act of violence, it was also a violation of the mind. I was nauseated when a man disregarded my pleas to stop injuring my body.

Rape is a taking from; it leaves a void and a feeling I cannot yet fully describe.

My body wasn't mine!

I learned that through personal violation.

My body was violated for the service of my father's fury, with physical consequences to me.

And by the silence that followed, too, and the pretending it didn't happen.

My body was used for my mother's safety and rescue, even when her sharp tongue emotionally ill-treated me during her drunken stupors.

And again, just like with my father, in the silence that followed, and the pretending it didn't happen.

My body was used by unknown men, seemingly theirs to take; their own wants and actions showed me so.

My parents took advantage of my body by trying to break my bones, tearing my skin, and obstructing my breathing until I blacked out.

Drunk, stinking older adults took advantage of my body.

So-called girlfriends' boyfriends took advantage of it, and babies, real lives, were created.

That was life.

My life!

Unsent Letter

To Nate

I hope you understand,

Like, properly understand,

How you wounded me.

-42-
The Numb Club

I did not choose trauma, depression, and anxiety. They all picked me. As did the men, all of those abusive men. How could I not have sustained deep wounds from the complex chaos in my life, and the catastrophes of 1-5-8 and beyond?

My emotional turmoil created long-lasting injuries. When these injuries are triggered and active, my nervous system and mind are deeply affected. However, there are times when my mind feels alive and totally coherent. It doesn't feel to me that I live in a permanent state of either depression or anxiety. They are part-time lodgers. When triggered into an active state, my nervous system and mind are deeply affected.

Trauma, depression, and anxiety are not feelings. Some say I will be better tomorrow, or I'm just having a bad day.

SCREAM

With zero medical training, I can describe what happens to my body when I am having a difficult time better than any other person can. I can't name the feelings as a medical professional can, but I know when they are active. I can describe what they feel like in my body.

Afterwards, I reflect to identify if I was wired, silent, or shaking from personal upset. Traumatic experiences block my memory, and old age contributes, making things even messier. I recognise and own my deficits, numbness, impulsive talking, or silence in the freeze when I become aware of them, often only after the fact.

I am a survivor of hellish experiences. In the last year, I've changed in many ways for the better, yet I sometimes slip into old patterns. This struggle is partly the result of fifty years of keeping secrets about abuse, leaving me feeling small, ashamed, embarrassed, and unworthy at times. Even with positive change, these patterns can persist.

If I had my time over again with the same scenarios, I would fight harder, be more physical with the men, and speak up immediately, not withholding to keep others safe. And not fear not being believed.

Imagining such a life brings hope and a sense of lightness.

There are times when I wonder about the conversations that happen when you are feeling downhearted, and people notice. The words they use are really something: what's wrong, smile, and my favourite, don't worry about it, be positive.

Are they saying not to worry when someone is down because it is wrong to be down, or is there something wrong with that person that makes them feel down?

Being down is a part of being a human with awareness. It helps us face chaos and recover. I've survived whatever life has brought, feeling it all. The pain isn't easy, but I believe things work out for me. Numbness, however, makes life lonelier.

Pain and suffering are standard parts of being human. I do my best to accept and expect this in my life.

Feelings are natural, and mine were intense for over fifty years, especially as a child at 1-5-8 facing danger, loneliness, homelessness, threats, violation, secrets, and seeking escape. These experiences shaped deep emotions and survival instincts.

This way of living made me highly aware of intense energy from a young age.

As an adult, I understand the power of crisis, having learned lessons and gained knowledge from fear and the experience of survival strategies. I intend never to push feelings away, knowing what I know now. I live through them, walking through every fire required of me when I can. This is hard work; I will never tame my insides, yet I give it my best when I can. I will continue my search for that medical specialist who can remove trauma from my body.

Delusional thinking, but still thinking it could happen. Man on the moon stuff, winning the lottery without a ticket kind of thinking.

As a child, I often puzzled over my tears. How could crying soothe me, even if nothing changed? Were my tears magic, carrying comfort?

Now I know tears hold real power. They are a potent balm, giving relief when we cry.

By doing the inner work and reading loads, I'm showing up differently now. Firstly, I'm permitting myself to be who I am, when I am, and how I am. Of course, I am also trying hard not to pretend anymore; I want to speak my truth.

Now I am one of the many women who show up in their
own lives with a more profound respect for ourselves.
I speak up and take up space in this world. I accept
the facts about my parents, family, and me, our lives of
confusion and ache.

I've come to accept that I wasn't equipped with the tools
I needed to protect myself as a young girl.

I was asked many years ago by a psychologist, "Who did
you go to, to speak about stuff, when you were little?
Things like being scared and other worries. Who listened
to you when you had a problem?"

I stared at her like she was speaking gibberish!

"No one, I went to no one, to speak with. No one
listened to me because I didn't ask them to; it wasn't
within my understanding to expect others to engage
with me or listen to my words. I was voiceless and
invisible. Un-hearable and un-expected-to-speak. I was
un-listenable to." Are children supposed to speak with
others, to tell them of their worries?

Because I suffered alone within the roles and rules of my
family, I understand things instinctively. As a frightened
kid with no one to help me navigate the world, no one to
speak up for me, and no one to talk to, a young girl in my
situation doesn't develop the crucial skills to understand
life and to find out who she is. I needed to discuss my life
with my parents. I needed them to witness my journey
and provide the fundamental principles that would help
me understand self-respect, loyalty, truth, protection,
support, and all the values parents are responsible for
teaching their children.

How does a child know what she likes, dislikes, wants or
not, feels or not, what is safe and what is not? How does

a kid work out who she is or how she wants to be in her life?

How does a traumatised kid know what questions to ask?

As I matured, I came to realise that the heaviness inside me stemmed from family circumstances. My childhood abilities were drained, leaving me unable to explore beyond my house. I didn't appear intellectually impaired, but I felt it. Not long ago, I asked a trusted medical professional why I struggled academically as a child, despite excelling in sports. How could I understand one and not the other? This question has haunted me.

Her gracious response, her kind, thoughtful, and loving way, was to let me know I wasn't mentally challenged but emotionally bled dry.

I know I was able to free my mind from the loop of draining emotions created by my home life and other frightening situations because running, swimming, and playing team sports helped me feel brighter and lighter. I felt energised during and after playing the sports I adored. It still bothers me today that I didn't have a sound mind in my younger days.

While I hold a deep understanding of my life's circumstances, I also see silver linings in a fear-filled childhood. Shifting between pain and perspective, I recognise the complex effects these experiences have had on me.

I read many articles about abuse and why people stay in places where they are not safe. Again, without formal training, my experience in my world showed me that people stay where they are familiar and feel at home, even in extreme difficulties.

Sometimes I hear people talk about celebration days like Mother's Day and conclude that we go to our family, the family we love, the familiarity of family and home, if it is what we know. If that is familiar, it's a pattern that we go back to, all the time, no question.

You will return to celebrate Mother's Day, to a difficult mother and a disastrous father, to a home of unhappy memories because it is familiar. I return to the pattern, to where my family was, and to the people who felt like home.

That was my pattern back then, always returning to the familiar. However, life has changed, and nowadays, I no longer returned to that place. Nor to those people.

I struggle to understand why people question those from painful families who return home. I sometimes feel set apart by society, misunderstood for seeking the comfort of the familiar. Is that so strange?

If you love your father and are told you cannot see him again or return to your family home to see him, how would that feel? How would you cope with that? Could you learn to numb yourself enough to forget him, your family home, and the comfort of your family traditions?

I carry deep thought patterns formed by the judgments I experienced in childhood. I have come to the conclusion that if children love their father, whether he is thunderous or not, then when we leave him and our familiar family home and comfort, we too need to return. I may not want to return to the dysfunction, but I want him, I want the house, my house, my bedroom, my stuff, my familiar, my neighbourhood, the two barky dogs two doors up, the kids next door, even the sounds of zsstt.

I wanted to return to the comfort of what I knew. What I learned was my home.

Ultimately, we must learn to love ourselves beyond what our parents can provide. They may want to love us, but they lack the know-how.

It helps me a great deal knowing that. Perhaps my parents wanted to love me, but lacked the capacity to show it.

I have learned that not being loved by a parent or parents, or by caregivers, cannot make one unlovable. But it can and does make us feel unloved.

Because they didn't show me love, I believed I was unlovable.

Now I know I am lovable, and okay exactly as I am, a profound realisation that has emerged in my healing journey.

In my experience, my parents were fighting their numerous demons so often that they didn't feel the love within themselves, so they couldn't give it to me. The way they showed love was not through words or affection. Their style of love was demonstrated by providing meals, my sporting gear, birthday presents, clothing, warm pyjamas, school uniforms, beach holidays, and lollies on Friday night.

The price of that kind of love, along with the cruelty and verbal abuse, was paid by my nervous system. No number of warm pajamas or bread and butter pudding could have matched caring, kindness, tenderness, and protection. This was clear to me, as I functioned in a state of hypervigilance, listening to and watching everything and every move, noting every word my parents said. I was always "on", clinging to the things that had kept me safe as a child, like holding onto an invisible rail to stay upright.

Changing life patterns can take a lifetime to overcome, if ever they can be.

I often feel in domestic abuse or abuse of any kind, the question isn't why we aren't loved.

The question, in my humble opinion, is whether I was protected.

And my answer to that is an unreserved, outright, definite, no! I was not protected.

-43-
Mr. Bilson

A lovely older gentleman appeared in my mother's life when I was fifteen. He seemed like a quiet, respectful man with a gentle demeanour and a full head of wild, curly brown hair. My mother and Mr. Bilson spent every waking moment together when they weren't at work. I was glad my mother seemed happy in her new relationship.

We had moved from our unit near the beach to another, still near the beach, yet closer to her new café job.

Mr. Bilson spent short chunks of time at our place, while my mother spent lots of time at Mr. Bilson's home.

On an ordinary weekday afternoon, while sitting in the lounge room watching TV, my mother suddenly announced she'd be back in the morning. Then she went out the front door. My mother got into the bright-coloured car of her new boyfriend, and off they went. My eyes followed her for a moment, unknowing, unprepared, surprised, scared. My head was spinning. It was 3.30pm That misery, all those mixed feelings, were left with me. Where does misery go? It goes inside your body, and that is what I carried.

Sometime around 7.30am, the next morning, my mother arrived home, got dressed in her work clothes, and drove off to work. Nothing was said about how I was feeling, what I had for dinner, or how my night alone had been.

A new low, a new learning of the way to manage my life without a parent in the house by myself. The nights alone became normal.

My mother arrived home from work, exhausted every day, and then dressed in her long nightgown. Over the top, she put on her dressing gown, put on her slippers, picked up her handbag and toiletry bag, and then walked out the door at 3.30pm to see the bright-coloured car waiting for her. In she got, and off they went.

That scenario went on five days a week, but weekends were a little different. My mother would come home sometime on Saturdays. It was usually around midday, or occasionally a bit later. Going upstairs to her bedroom, she collected a new set of clothing while Mr. Bilson waited downstairs in our lounge room. These were the brief periods he spent in our unit.

My mother, with her handbag, toiletries bag, and a new set of clothes, would then tell Mr Bilson she was ready, and together they got into his outrageously bright-coloured car and off they went.

I'd always longed to live in silence in the years living at 1-5-8 Lavandar Avenue, and now that I had that, it felt very lonely.

Once again, I accepted this situation, having to pretend my life was okay and to smile at the right time when Mr. Bilson came in the door. I smiled at every smile from my mother; I thought I should. I smiled at every smile from my friends when they asked how I was doing, yet it was all just an act, a pretence. There were many things about my mother's relationship with Mr. Bilson that I once felt so happy about, but now I felt were inexplicably wrong.

The selfishness, the lack of parental responsibility, and their pursuit of being together every evening, seven days a week, filled me with pangs of profound guilt, as if I were worth nothing. I felt alone. Was I worth one night, a few nights? I thought I still needed mothering and nurturing. My mother had no idea I was hurting, zero clue.

One of the most striking instances of this lack of awareness was on weekends, when she would return to collect new clothing. A fleeting visit and gone, like a magician's rabbit in his hat. Disappearance 101. Mother, are you actually a magician? Because it feels like you are to me. Being childless was seemingly her life's goal; she gave birth, and then the child should disappear at the snap of her fingers, just like magic, making it all possible. I'm positive she actually yearned to be childless, but now she had a new child, Mr. Bilson's son, who wasn't hers, and she spent time with him. Why replace me? I was actually hers!

On a strangely awkward Saturday afternoon, Mr. Bilson dropped my mother off at home and returned thirty minutes later to pick her up. My mother, waiting for him, seated at the kitchen table, told me how heartbreaking it was to see Mr. Bilson's difficult teenage son act out. He would yell at his father and ignore any direction. My mother told me how tough it was for poor Mr. Bilson to have to live like that.

She unwrapped the whole saga of how hard Mr. Bilson's life was and the efforts he was making in his home and with his family to improve their lives, including his own. Despite Mr. Bilson doing everything for his son, the son still couldn't appreciate having a loving father.

I listened. I was quiet as I saw pain in my mother's eyes and agony in her heart for poor Mr. Bilson. She said she would spend as much time with Mr. Bilson as he needed to make him feel appreciated and loved. She wanted to guide his difficult son on the right path in life. This included cooking their favourite delicious meals and watching TV together in their warm, comfortable lounge room with a big colour TV. She was going to help them be a connected, loving family.

I felt both jealous and sad. Then my guilt over that jealousy overwhelmed me, keeping me from speaking up for myself. I nodded at my mother's sad Mr. Bilson and his difficult son, stories.

Did my mother not see, in any way, what she was doing in sharing that story with me, that she was leaving me alone, her daughter, to concentrate on giving her attention and support to another child?

Hell, Mother: while you're at his place, guiding, leading conversation, cooking for, caring for, sitting with, and talking to Mr. Bilson and his son, you yourself have a lonely, vulnerable daughter in your own house, alone! With no one talking to me, watching TV with me, and no one caring for me. No one is looking out for me, 24/7.

Her own child, who needed to be rebuilt from the inside out, required certainty and a family unit to feel whole again, needed surety that she was loved and would always be protected. I needed to know that the promise of the life I left behind at 1-5-8 Lavandar Avenue would remain in my past, and my new beachside life would be one where I could depend on my mother for love, support, care, and understanding.

I didn't say any of this to my mother. It still wasn't in me to do so. I wish I'd had the courage to speak up, but I didn't. I could not get the words out.

Same me, same freeze pattern.

How could my mother think it was okay to give to another family, seven nights and two days every week, her attention and support, leaving nothing of her to her own child? Her daughter, still traumatised, having lived through what she had lived through, torment and debilitating fear and neglect year after year?

For the millionth time in my young life, this situation made no sense to me. I felt nothing but total confusion about loyalty, total bewilderment about parental love and her lack of constancy towards her own child.

If Mr. Bilson's family came first in his life, would it not make sense that my mother's family would come first in her life? That question raised so many more questions in me!

Just exactly what sort of man was Mr. Bilson, I wondered. Was he the gentle, cheerful man that he initially appeared to be? Was he a thoughtful, kind man? He couldn't possibly be, as he would not allow a woman to leave her young daughter alone so often. Frightened and fragile at just fifteen years of age. I know Mr. Bilson wanted my mother, and my mother wanted him; that was that. I was not in their equation.

I wanted my mother to be with me; I wanted to be a family unit when we left our father. Yet with all the behaviours that my mother had displayed and was displaying, all the sad stories of her life, the behaviours in her drinking, and now the betrayal of me, still I did not

give up on the hope that she would indeed one day make
me a priority.

I was completely unaware of what a truly secure family
should look like or what children should expect from
their family members. However, I knew my mother was
the only adult who provided me with a home and food.
And now she was absent; I lost the certainty she had
promised, and with it, the assurance.

The next afternoon, Mr. Bilson came inside our house
as my mother was getting ready to go back to his place.
He sat down on a dining room chair and called me to sit
with him. This was a first.

He began by saying, "My dear, I think you could be doing
more for your mother, doing more around the house to
make her feel like she matters when she comes home.
Show her you appreciate her."

He continued asking me to make her feel better when
she came home in the afternoons, even though it meant
doing more for myself. Mr. Bilson pointed to me, telling
me I should be doing my own washing, sweeping the
floors, cooking meals, and taking care of myself; I was
old enough.

"Your mother works hard all week, and she shouldn't
have to come home and look after you, when you are
quite capable of looking after yourself," argued Mr.
Bilson.

I remember looking at the floor, feeling so ashamed,
feeling like I had let my mother down, let myself down,
in that moment. I felt Mr. Bilson was right when he said
he loved my mother and that he could see how exhausted
she was. I realised I could do more to make my mother

feel at ease when she came back home, so I took his advice to heart.

That night, after my deep agonising guilt and shame had begun to subside and my thinking brain kicked back into working order, I started to rehash the stern talking-to from Mr. Bilson. And I realised I already did my own washing, folding, and putting my clothes away. I already swept the floors, made my bed, and ensured the house was tidy. My mother bought food, and I organised meals.

And...I began to smile.

What! Me? Do the right thing by my mother...? What?

Any guilt and shame for not caring well enough for my mother flowed from my body that evening. My mother, along with her boyfriend, Mr. Bilson, left me alone for almost two years. I struggle to find the right words to express the absence of words and a mother.

I think it's a combination of two things that continue to compound the hurt:

- Broken trust; trust that was never developed, never earned; I never knew how to hold trust, a problem when you live a life of betrayal and trauma. When you hurt so often and so painfully, trust is an illusion.

- Secondly, it seems to me I tried to mother myself, making my own decisions, yet I was frightened if they were the right decisions. Second-guessing myself became the norm.

Unsent Letter

To the woman who lives in the same unit as me

I do not know you anymore

I don't want to know you anymore

In this model

You become meaner and more selfish

by the week

You should never have been

given a child to raise

I'm going to report you to someone who cares about kids.

Unsent Letter

To the Pretender,

Mr Bilson,

I cannot like you.

Not for who you were, and not for what you allowed.

I cannot like the way you stood by and accepted my mother's treatment of me. I cannot like the way you occupied space and authority without ever using it to protect. You didn't have to hurt me directly to be part of the harm. You just had to stay silent. And you did.

You arrived loudly in my life.

And you left loudly, too.

Your big, ridiculous orange V8 announced itself long before you did. Everyone knew when you were coming. Everyone knew when you were leaving. The engine roared, bubbled, shook the air, and made sure no one missed the moment.

Honestly, you may as well have arranged a fanfare.

A brass section. A drum roll. Maybe a trumpet or two, just to be certain the whole street understood the message: not just arriving, leaving.

And leaving meant I was staying.

Did you ever think about that?

Did you ever think that people hearing that car pull away might think, Oh. That kid's alone again? Another night. Another departure. Another adult choosing movement over responsibility.

Or did it not occur to you at all?

That car made me feel exposed. Like the entire neighbourhood could hear my mother being taken somewhere else. Like my being left behind had a soundtrack. Loud. Unavoidable. Public.

The exhaust rattled and growled and demanded attention, and I remember thinking how unfair it was that something so unnecessary could take up so much space, while I was expected to take up none.

You never noticed that.

Or you noticed and didn't care.

That car wasn't just a transport. It was volume. It was dominance. It was a spectacle. And every time it pulled away, it reminded me that leaving could be loud and unapologetic while staying required silence.

So no, I don't like you.

And I don't like your stupid car either.

Not because it was orange.

Not because it was a V8.

But because it announced a choice that was never made for me.

I know what you weren't thinking.

That much is obvious.

But what, exactly, did you think you were doing?

This letter will never be sent.

You don't need to read it.

I just needed to say it.

-44-
Hamster Wheels

It was a cold, windy winter evening, around 5pm. The grey light pressed against the rooftops like a heavy hand, and the house felt smaller than usual, as if it was shrinking around me. I was home alone when the knock came, the one I had been told to expect, yet I still wasn't prepared for it. My mother had said he would arrive at five to look at the washing machine.

I told myself it was just a repairman. Just a washing machine.

Even after everything that had come before, part of me still wanted to believe that. When I opened the door, he looked ordinary, not threatening, not strange. Just a man at the end of his workday, tired, maybe overworked, the kind of man you wouldn't notice twice in a crowd. Casually dressed, clean, polite. His ordinariness was almost disarming. And that was the trick of it, the ordinary always was. Pretending! Was he?

My chest tightened, a subtle warning spreading beneath my ribs, sharp, automatic, familiar like tiny claws digging inward, a pulse of unease racing through my veins. But my mind dismissed it. Not another one. Not today. Not any day! I told myself I was overreacting. I told myself this visit was unorthodox in timing, yes, but normal in purpose. Washing machine. Repairs. Tools. Nothing else. Please, be nothing else.

And yet, the hamster wheel in my body churned, faster this time, racing through what I knew could happen, what I had survived before, spinning circuits I never chose to enter.

He stepped inside, nodded politely, and sat at the kitchen table as though he belonged there. I made toasted sandwiches for my dinner. The butter hissed on the hotplate; the smell of toast spread through the room. When he cheekily asked for one, I laughed lightly, a trained reflex, not amusement.

Something in me flinched at the boldness of that request. A tiny bell rang in the back of my skull. I ignored it. I didn't want to believe what I had learned to expect.

We talked as we ate, our voices level, almost friendly.

I wanted ordinary.

I wanted quiet.

I wanted this visit to be what my mother said it was.

I walked to the lounge, expecting the hum of the washing machine, the clank of tools, the ordinary domestic soundscape of repairs.

But he followed, close; too close.

And suddenly, the air around me shifted.

I stiffened, not from fear, but from recognition. My skin prickled, pulse quickened, every nerve already rehearsing

the choreography that my body remembered from that
old, unholy routine before my thoughts could catch up.
My chest tightened again. This time, I recognised it.

Another again.

Another man.

Another performance. By me, acting 101.

I kept thinking the same thing over and over: if my
mother were here, this wouldn't happen. She wouldn't let
it. Part of me longed for her return, a hope that someone
I semi-trusted might walk through the door and make
it all stop. And yet, another part of me recoiled at the
thought, embarrassed, ashamed, unsure how I could
even begin to explain. How could I tell her what was
happening in her absence? The contradictions twisted in
my chest, a mix of longing and dread, wanting her here
and not here at the same time.

I remembered the others, the knock at the door, the
footsteps in the hall, the smell of aftershave, cigarettes,
sweat, the shifting eyes, the "polite" smiles. So many
men arriving under the guise of something else. So many
ordinary beginnings that slid into something unthinkable.

No matter how many times it happened, the realisation
hit like cold water: Oh. He's not here for the washing
machine. He's here for me.

A truth too unorthodox to speak aloud.

A truth too bizarre to belong in any everyday world.

He smiled and said, "Everything's been organised,
everything's okay."

A line rehearsed. Used and worn out from repetition.

Everything wasn't okay. And my body knew it long before I let my mind admit it.

He stayed close behind me. His arms wrapped tightly around my waist, confidently. As I led him to the double bed, my mother's walls seemed to hum, not with sound, but with memory. The scent of stale cigarettes mixed with her perfume, a cocktail of secrets. The air grew thick, clinging to my skin like damp cloth.

Every step I took was deliberate and controlled; each toe, calf, and shoulder instinctively knew its role. A practiced dance, a role I never auditioned for, but my muscles had memorised, with every fibre coiled and ready before my mind could protest.

Would he threaten to choke me?

Would he slap me in the face?

Would he crawl over me, painfully, carelessly, as if I wasn't human?

And would I care?

Did I even have the capacity left to care?

By then, the caring had long since been wrung out of me.

When he finished what he came to do, his breath lingered in the room; hot, heavy, sour. I only let myself breathe again when he zipped his trousers and looked away. For a moment, he seemed almost sorry, or maybe just embarrassed. It didn't seem to matter, yet his feelings affected me. What happened to me that made me worry about him, not myself? Regardless of the damage.

When the door finally closed behind him, the silence was deafening, as it had been cultivated in my mind.

The house returned to its standard shape, but I did not.

I curled into myself on the bed, trembling, staring at the ceiling. The disbelief weighed down on me like an unshakeable burden. Tears fell quietly, exhausted. My mind replayed every act, every scene of this horrific play.

I was so exhausted, exhausted in a way sleep couldn't fix.

Then, the thought hit me hard: another perfect performance by me.

Another survival. Another act. One more scene in the theatre I never chose to perform in.

I stepped into the shower, letting the water scorch my skin until it turned red, each droplet stinging like tiny pins. Steam blurred the mirror, and my reflection faded into a ghostly echo. Muscles that had learned to flinch, coil, and guard now shivered under the heat, instinct and memory working faster than thought, with each fibre trained to stay tense and alert.

Later, I sat on the veranda under the night sky. I wished for anything that might numb the pain: alcohol, drugs, oblivion, forgetfulness.

Even through the silence, exhaustion, and shame, a familiar and miraculous truth pulsed within me:

I was still alive.

Not strangled this time.

Not broken.

Still performing.

Still surviving the behaviours drilled into me at the theatre of 1-5-8.

Still the men.

Always the men.

I didn't fully realise it at first, not consciously. After so many men, the pattern should have been clear, but it wasn't. Until him.

He was different, probably in his late twenties or even early thirties, clean-shaven, and almost boyish in his hesitation. There was a hesitation in how he stood at the door, a carefulness that didn't match his purpose. His eyes flicked around the room as if he wasn't sure he was in the right place. Tentative. Polite. Almost nervous.

And I now saw he didn't understand how to behave, unlike the others, not with the same certainty or confrontational confidence.

He acted differently. Not urgent, not forceful.

It seemed almost human, strange amidst everything that came before.

He followed me enthusiastically to the bedroom at first, as if he wanted what he came for right then, yet there was no harshness or assurance.

Once he stepped back, staring into my eyes, the room's tension shifted unexpectedly.

I cried softly in my mother's bed, tears stinging my eyes, burning my cheeks, my chest heaving in little spasms, my pulse pounding like a warning drum. Everything around me pressed into that moment like a living witness. The sheets smelled faintly of perfume, a floral sweetness clashing with the harsh tang of cigarettes. The overflowing ashtray on the side table spilled onto the polished wood, smudges of grey and white like tiny ghosts. The room still held the residual warmth of the day, but it felt heavy, thick with the scent of smoke, skin, and long-kept secrets.

He froze. His face turned shy, embarrassed, almost childlike in confusion. A man stripped of his script, suddenly unsure of what he had just done.

And then something inside me shifted; something I still can't fully explain.

I felt sorry for him.

Or maybe I saw a reflection of something in me.

His embarrassment.

His discomfort.

His sudden uncertainty.

It tangled with my shame, my confusion; raw nerves touching.

For a moment, I wondered if he knew.

Suppose he sensed that something was wrong. If he suspected I hadn't been expecting him for anything other than the washing machine repairs.

He dressed quickly, head bowed, like someone who
had wandered into a story he didn't understand. A man
expecting one thing, finding another, a trembling girl
instead of what he thought he would see.

And in that fragile, awkward silence, the shock hit me
again:

He didn't know that I didn't know what he had come for.

It seemed to me we were both lost in something neither of
us could identify.

Unsent Letter

Dear Me

Not all is lost-

You might find a silver lining at last.

You've learned at 1-5-8

the intricacies of performance theatre

Acting 101, pretending 101,

Yay Me but still, a Sad Face.

-45-

Holding Onto The Rail

Even in the quiet after that night, my body still remembered the chaos. Every nerve, every fibre, remained coiled, ready, rehearsing survival the way it always had. And yet, in the stillness, I began noticing the small things I could reach for, literal or not, to keep myself steady: a handrail, a shelf, the constant grip of someone else beside me. Holding on became more than instinct; it became a lifeline, a quiet ritual that reminded me survival didn't always demand vigilance or performance. Sometimes, it demanded nothing more than staying present, anchoring myself to something solid while the world spun too fast.

A few months ago, I rode the bus to a large shopping centre about thirty minutes from home. The driver sped along, faster than felt safe, the engine growling as the bus swayed. My stomach tightened with every sharp turn. A few passengers called out to him to slow down, but he didn't; if anything, it seemed he pressed the accelerator harder.

I moved closer to an older woman who was gripping the rail so tightly that her knuckles had gone white. I sat beside her and held her trolley with one hand, steadying her with the other when the bus lurched. Soon I found myself gripping the rail too, the metal vibrating under my

267

palm, anchoring me as the driver sped through traffic as if we were in a race.

By the time we reached our stop, both of us were shaky. We stepped off the bus with a shared sense of relief. We laughed, almost nervously, grateful for the handrail that kept us steady when the journey became chaotic. Holding onto that cool, solid metal had kept us tethered, preventing the panic from taking over. Strange as it sounded, the physical act of gripping the rail brought a sense of calm after the frantic ride.

Then it happened again. The lesson is to hold on!

At a crowded football game last month, everyone around us was tense as the score kept changing. A man in the front row noticed how often we stood up and sat down in anxiety.

"Grab onto the rail; it'll steady your nerves," he called out as he stood up. "Hold the rail, hold the rail, when things get tough, cling to that bloody rail."

We laughed at his antics as he swayed back and forth. His knuckles went white as he clung onto the rail like it was his lifesaver.

It was then that I realised how meaningful the phrase "holding the rail" was. The recent bus trip with the too-fast driver showed me how clinging to something solid, literally the rail, could offer a sense of control. Now, in the football stadium with the footy fanatic, the same physical act became a way to steady ourselves during tense moments. The phrase "holding the rail" began to resonate as a metaphor for finding security and steadiness in stressful situations, both on the bus and at the match.

This connection brought my past into focus, with the metaphor of "holding onto the rail" revealing how much I cling to what feels safe and familiar. My parents had their own virtual rails: the survival strategies they gripped during their childhoods. Like them, I held onto the rails, my coping mechanisms, for a sense of security.

Was the holding on still servicing my behaviours now? Had I let go at all? Had my parents let go of any of their holding on or did they continue to hold on, acting out what had kept them safe in childhood into their adult lives?

My father fought for himself, always on guard. He never found peace, clinging to survival even when it no longer served him.

My mother held on by drinking and smoking from age twelve to fit in. She did what her family and his friends wanted, giving of herself to survive. Her coping allowed her to numb the pain from repeated abuse.

My parents carried their childhood survival tactics into adulthood. Even when it hurt them, that was how they knew to survive.

My mother's family used bold survival tactics, fighting for basics and numbing themselves against pain. They faced harsh choices: find a way to get by, or be institutionalised.

These men, now gone, had honed their survival skills throughout their lives. Letting go felt too risky; traumatised children often lack the courage to abandon the rails that once kept them safe.

Holding on to my rail, both literally and metaphorically, has served me well in the past, helping me survive difficult experiences. Yet I now wonder, do I still require the same strategies, the same kind of holding on, to feel safe?

In some families, children without a father in the home were taken to institutions and treated like criminals simply because their father left the family. They will be excused for holding on, in my humble opinion.

-46-
Sticky Love

Even after learning to steady myself, to hold onto something solid when the world spun too fast, I began to notice the quiet ways my family had done the same. The rails weren't always literal; sometimes they were a hand to hold, a routine to follow, a meal shared, a holiday ritual, or the gentle smile of a parent. These small, steadying acts became anchors, moments that tethered me to belonging, safety, and love. They were the glue that held us together, the sticky love that shaped my childhood, even amid the chaos.

We shared some relaxed, joyful moments, and they felt as if I were part of a real family. It did feel that way for a short time. The safe, smiling, relaxed times are the memories I recall. Those times felt like sticky love, like they were the "sticky family love glue" that kept us together!

The family came together to celebrate important moments. My parents showed their love by weaving it into our family traditions, and I feel the same love woven into my story. I hope you can feel it, too.

When it came to meals, my father always had an enormous appetite! Fortunately, my mother was a highly skilled and creative cook who especially enjoyed making our evening meals. The dinners were always large and flavourful, which made my father especially happy and satisfied. We enjoyed a wide variety of red and white meats, fish, and even specialties like tripe and brains, all of which everyone at the table enjoyed, not. My mother's spaghetti Bolognese was a favourite of mine, as were her casserole and dumplings, dishes I haven't tasted since she last made them.

I cannot remember the full array of desserts after each meal, yet some stand out: bread and butter pudding, baked rice pudding, and plum pudding, always topped with homemade custard. Other nights brought jelly tarts with pastry lace and sides of whipped cream and ice cream.

Let me, for one moment, return to the mention of custard. There was, in fact, a custard issue! My favourite dessert was my mother's runny, lump-free custard, always tested before serving and always perfect. Thank you, Mum, for your patience in making this much-awaited dessert.

My mother always served my father exactly what he wanted, ensuring we had delicious meals each evening. It required significant effort, yet she did it for us!

On holidays, we went on regular camping trips. Visits to the coastline and Ari Bay were my father's favourite fishing and surfing spots, and eventually became our family's favourites as well. I loved those holidays, living inside our large green canvas tent that always smelled distinctively like vacation. The centre pole was a highlight; it made the tent feel huge, almost like a circus tent, and we lived there for three weeks. My bunk beds were set on one side, my parents' double bed on the other, and the kitchen area was by the entrance, where my mother mainly cooked the fish my father caught during his daily outings. Our impressive tent was one in a row of family friends' tents, which made the holidays even more fun. The main activity was fishing, mainly when the fathers fished off the surf beach, and it was the highlight for everyone.

Most mornings, the families staying in the tents met outside to discuss plans for the day: barbecue lunches in the park, swimming, running up and down dunes, or waiting for the milk van to buy small bottles of flavoured milk. I enjoyed our group activities, and, like the other kids, I ran and swam in the surf. We fished in the creeks with smaller rods, playing until exhaustion and sun-kissed skin was our reward. Every night after an early dinner, we all returned to the beach. Watching the fathers cast their fishing lines into the waves at dusk was exciting. I loved sitting on the sand at dusk, watching the sun go down, as we chatted and laughed together.

I vividly remember the anglers using large yellow torches to fix their fishing rods, especially when lines became tangled in the dark. With so many people fishing, lines often got crossed, and the torches made it easier to untangle the mess. Helping each other untangle lines was an evening ritual filled with laughter among friends, making it feel like one big happy family where everyone belonged. It truly felt like a family holiday.

Our family always celebrated, thanks to my parents, who gave gifts for birthdays, Christmas, and Easter. Each year, we went to the Ekka as a family. It was my favourite event. I couldn't sleep the night before. On Tuesday, we'd leave home about 10am. On arrival, my father showed us the police station in case we got lost and checked our coats in. I rode every ride I wanted. We visited all the animal pavilions, touching almost every animal, and bought sample bags. After collecting our coats, we ate ham sandwiches and hot chips, then watched the horse-

and-chariot races, smash-up cars, clowns, and fireworks in the main ring. Ekka Day was always filled with eagerness, laughter, and cold wind, a truly favourite day of my childhood.

Even amidst the chaos of 1-5-8 Lavandar Avenue they offered moments of light and opportunity. My parents, in their own way, tried to give me experiences that nurtured my growth and curiosity. They enrolled me in gymnastics, where I could stretch, tumble, and discover the strength of my own body. Art classes let me express myself through painting and drawing, capturing what my words could not always convey. Dance brought rhythm, solitude, tenderness of movement, plus absolute joy, while sport gave me energy, teamwork, and a sense of achievement.

I felt lucky when my father took me shopping for new sports gear. Despite having little money, he ensured I had the necessary equipment for softball, netball, and swimming. There were softball cleats, gloves, bats, balls, swimsuits, bathing caps, towels, flippers, goggles, netball shoes, and uniforms.

My father knew the family who owned a nearby sports store and had an account there. Each year, he helped choose my sporting gear, as we discussed sports and competitions. He always said I should be fully equipped to succeed. During trainings and competitions, I felt like the luckiest girl with my new sports gear.

Family dinners out were always a treat. My father began this habit when I was about seven. Some Fridays, he drove us to Wynnum for fish and chips for dinner. It was always wrapped in clean white butcher's paper, making the whole event feel extra special. Especially when my mother made large cones from white paper, filling them to the brim with hot, crunchy chips and fish pieces. It was special to eat together in the park this way.

After our meal, I played on the swings in the park until dusk! It was a peaceful time that I remember with a smile and warmth in my heart. Dusk was a time associated with fun back then. I still adore dusk.

On other Friday nights, my father took me to a lolly shop nearby, then at home, would tip the filled lolly bag onto the kitchen table. With us both seated on chairs, elbows on the table, he shared the lollies out. My father smiled a lot on these outings, and I felt a flutter of excitement, hoping he would smile more often.

We sometimes went out to dinner on the weekends too. One of their favourite restaurants was a seafood restaurant at Wynnum. Sometimes on a Sunday, we would visit a restaurant that looked like a small, beautiful, freshly painted old house. "Williams" was also at Wynnum, serving the most delicious freshly caught seafood, always paired with the tastiest ripe red tomatoes. I felt spoiled visiting restaurants as a child; I thought that I didn't deserve to enjoy such delicious food, served by others, yet I adored the feeling of being together as a happy family.

The public face and smile of my father were truly something to behold, given that, at those times, he was unrecognizable from the bloke who lived at 1-5-8. My father's public demeanour was splendidly friendly and good-humoured, sociable, and welcoming. He was the first to greet everyone he met, compliment the waitstaff on the fabulous food, and engage in friendly small talk with guests in restaurants. His response to any enquiry of "how are you, Len" was a boisterously delightful "bloody marvellous!" My father would repeat this sentence, always following up with a firm pat on the back and his beaming smile. He tried to inspire others to be happy, too, though I knew at times his big, beaming smile wasn't entirely genuine. Something made me think it was, and it was at those times that I felt sorry for my father, and I felt happy for him too, as he tried to make himself and others feel good about themselves, the day, or the company. In his public life, the people he encountered without a smile always caught his attention.

In public, my father looked almost unrecognizable from the man at home. Outside, he was friendly, sociable, and charming. My father was an entertainer, wearing his big smile and laughing with his larger-than-life laugh. I realised early in my childhood that this cheerful entertainer was not the father I knew; he was my father, who was smiling big smiles. My father told jokes, laughed his big laugh, danced, and sang. He spent time in nursing homes entertaining the audience, which was truly his jam, the Entertainer, the Actor, the Pretender, doing what he loved.

In those moments, he was an entertainer, a man with a contagious laugh and larger-than-life energy. The chatty, singing, dancing comedian I saw and was always hoping the real smiling man in public would follow us home.

Those are just a few of the many generous and caring moments that make our good times special. They are in my memory bank, cherished and grateful for each one.

For Always.

The Photo Reminder

Those anchors of sticky love and family routines have carried me far, but they could not prevent the past from resurfacing. Life has a way of reminding me that the rails I once clung to, even the people I clung fast to, and the love I had experienced were only part of the story. Sometimes, memories return with a force that the present can barely contain.

As an adult, while navigating my primary school's website, I was chatting with a year seven classmate who sent me a newspaper article with a photo of me from when I was thirteen.

The article discussed my close call in a drowning incident in huge seas. I remember the event. I felt nothing during the online discussion, but the memory of being rescued and taken to the hospital eventually returned vividly.

However, the next week, looking at the photo again, I found myself in excruciating pain, sobbing, screaming, unable to breathe at times. I rang my closest friend and cried and yelled to her, at the top of my screaming voice.

The photo showed me exactly who I was at thirteen years of age, just one month before the first time I was...sent with a man for his use of my body.

To see that photo of me brought not just the harrowing experience of my prostitution into perspective, the picture in my hand showed me exactly who the men were being given as a sex toy.

I was staring at a young girl, an innocent child, someone I did not recognise. I had forgotten what she looked like, the innocence she carried at that age, the sadness in her eyes, and her shyness. Seeing myself in the photograph sent me into a spiral, my whole body spinning with rage and nausea so profound that I completely lost any sense of stability. I was crying hysterically, sobbing as I yelled about how anyone could hand over that shy, innocent young girl to men for abuse and exploitation.

How could any man think it was okay to meet for sex with such a young girl? The photo's image brought the reality back to me, not just the memory, but the actual girl, seeing her again after many years.

The neighbours heard my hysteria and knocked on my front door, calling out to make sure I was okay. I let them know I was.

I was not in any state of mind or body to speak the awful truths that this photo had reminded me of.

It was the most un-drug-induced, incoherent, lost-in-hysteria moment I had ever experienced.

Speaking with my Sista Rose-Ann helped me enormously. She knew I was in trouble emotionally and physically, listening and "more listening", then talking to me the way a true friend would. Eventually, I calmed enough to notice that my head ached so badly I needed to hang up the telephone and go to bed.

Even in the midst of that raw, shattering moment, I felt, deep down, the faint echo of the anchors that had carried me through childhood: the sticky love of family dinners, the steadying rails of holidays and routines, the quiet, unnoticed ways I had been held. Those memories didn't erase the pain, but they reminded me that I had survived before, that I could still find a grip, however small, to steady myself in the chaos of memory and emotion. The rails of care, love, and resilience were still there, invisible yet present, guiding me through even the most turbulent storms.

Unsent Letter

Dear Me

You didn't die in the wild seas' incident.

You didn't die

You wanted to die

But you didn't.

-48-
Puzzling Pieces

A word stronger than inconceivable is needed to describe the person and actions involved in managing the prostitution of an underage teen.

The actions were: Implausible, Unthinkable, Unimaginable, Ludicrous, Unbelievable, Absurd, Preposterous, Outrageous, Contemptible, Shocking, Obscene, Lewd, Shameful, Offensive, Staggering, Repulsive, Heinous, Atrocious, Inexcusable, Abysmal, Sickening, and Horrifying.

The person acted in a way that was: Appalling, Immoral, Disgraceful, Indecent, Corrupt, Depraved, Sinful, Iniquitous, Monstrous, Evil, Malevolent, Discreditable, Malicious, Criminal, Abominable, Dishonourable, Devious, Fraudulent, Lying, Cunning, Faithless, Cheating, Falsehearted, and Despicable.

Why was I the target of the many men who violated my body? I have wondered this for more than half my lifetime.

Who allowed the men access to me, and why?

What was the person gaining?

Did they understand what I was losing? What I lost permanently?

For many decades, I asked myself what was I doing so wrong, even unknowingly, to be the girl who was set upon, set up to be used, raped? How did they know they were going to be accepted by me for their sexual use and abuse of my body? The confusion consumed me for years, with answers eluding me as I tried to piece everything together. On the other end of the spectrum, there were also decades when I had no memory, no thoughts of the events. Thank goodness a mind and a soul can rescue us and keep us safe when required.

The pieces of the jigsaw, upon returning, came as quick moments, visions like flashbacks, fleeting thoughts over the years. Each fragment brought me closer to understanding.

The crisp white shirt with the stiff white collar...the crisp white shirt...the crisp white shirt...

The long, narrow staircase...my blue dress...the act...one man leaving the room...

The...urgency in the kiss...the urgency...made me angry.

The blue suit coat...

the voice Hello..., the kiss on my head...

Unbelievable, the most unbelievable coincidences! Surely it was not just my being in the wrong place at the wrong time for me, but the right place and time for each of those men.

Greg? No way! How on earth did he know where I lived?

The man, the teacher I knew, standing on the footpath outside my house.

Was it a stalker who wasn't Greg? That would make some kind of sense, but what was their purpose, their gain?

The Tradie? How did I end up alone in the house when he arrived! Alone...when a man arrived wanting sex. He knew what he was coming to do, but I did not. Did he see that in my eyes, as his look was one of confusion afterwards!

Mr. Bilson thought it was okay to leave me alone, his new girlfriend's daughter! Another's daughter was alone in her home, even though she was desperate for her mother to be with her.

What was written on my face, in my body language, that said, Come, abuse me, stalk me, treat me like a worthless being? These questions looped in my mind, my thoughts confused and perplexed. I realised I was utterly traumatised.

Time alone in a mental health clinic brought the trauma inside me to the surface. Maybe medication helped, or perhaps I was finally in safe hands.

I was now a whole person, not half a kid, not half a woman, but one whole person with a properly thinking brain: no longer the taxed, drained brain, the crushed mind from the Theatre of 1-5-8. I was here, finally present as a fully thinking living human being, as I was meant to be.

Slowly, over the years, those painful memories began to return more often. Decades on, after unimaginable cruelty had stolen from me and numbed my brain, the jigsaw puzzle of my life finally came together, restoring the memories once lost.

Decades on from those events, I moved forward in time and a significant change occurred.

By February 17, 2021, I entered a new phase of change. Years after the abuse and its aftermath, I was suffering ongoing pain from an injury I sustained in 2020. During my recovery from this recent injury, I fell into a deep depression. Initially, the depression medication worked for a few months but then stopped being effective.

By 2021, some four months into taking the new medication, I began to feel frightening side effects. The side effects were dreaming of suicidal scenarios. I had the same dream for four consecutive nights: flying over a bridge in a glider suit, then plunging into the water and dying on impact. Waking from the dreams, I felt overwhelmed.

On the fifth day, I woke from the same nightmare, sat up, and began planning my death. I felt neither overwhelmed nor at ease with this ending.

Knowing I lacked a glider suit, I planned to drive my car onto the bridge and over the side. I dressed for the day as usual. As I walked to the garage, I paused, thinking of my children. They had good lives, good jobs, and knew they were loved. I thought they would be okay.

I got into my car, put the keys in the ignition, and realised I didn't have my phone.

Going back inside to get my phone, I suddenly realised my children would be left without a mother, just as I had lived. They would have to live out their lives alone, missing the care only a loving mother can give. I knew that pain.

I understood the deepest pain this way of life could create.

I stopped moving.

Then I phoned my GP to tell her my story. An ambulance arrived, taking me to the local hospital's emergency department. There, I was attended to by two nurses throughout my stay in that ward. Admitted, consulted, and monitored, two on one for five hours, I was escorted to the psychiatric centre by two huge security guards, one walking in front and one walking behind me. I was petrified and ashamed.

There I stayed for eight days. The medication was reviewed, and changes were made to suit me much better. My complex PTSD and depression diagnosis required medication, so medication remained, a new one. Thank goodness for psychiatrists, as my new medicines did not give me side effects of wanting to take my life. I am beyond grateful, as I could have been dead before I realised it was a plan with failings and misgivings.

The hospital staff were kind and supportive. However, it took this frightening experience to realise I'd reached my lowest point that I could recall.

The psychiatric team worked behind safety glass with locked doors, but our room doors remained open. It was an experience, even for a risk-taker like me.

I met with the psychiatrist and registrar who invested in my well-being.

The attending psychiatrist told me my GP was arranging my admission into a private Mental Health Clinic for further treatment upon my release.

Having a caring, supportive GP is the difference. This is the person who made things happen for me. I was booked into a mental health facility for three weeks.

The OC

Eight days later, I left for new treatment in private care. The people there, like those I'd met the week before, struggled with different mental health issues. The clinic was quieter than the hospital, yet it was always busy.

Living at the clinic felt like a resort, offering comfort, privacy, and attentive service. For the first three days, a nurse checked on me every fifteen minutes. The same psychiatrist, registrar, and I met in daily consultations.

My door would close whenever I wanted it to. I felt safe.

Therapy sessions lasted up to five hours a day, and meals were prepared from real food. It was the best holiday, a respite from life's stressors, that helped me feel grounded in my recovery.

I had visits from nurses, cleaners, patients, the social worker, and the registrar, so I never felt alone.

The first thing the psychiatrist did was talk about my frightening reaction to the medication, which led to my plan to take my life. The medication was again reviewed and, thank goodness, was changed to suit me, and I have never felt better. I landed the best psychiatrist the first time around; although our connection wasn't immediate, it grew quickly.

Continuing the daily talk therapy felt too much at times. I was always met with kind-hearted encouragement, and I felt stimulated to write every day whilst hospitalised. I found it surprisingly easy in the quiet environment. I saw so much more in this type of therapy than I had found in my usual journaling. I think it was the fact that there was a trusted doctor who was invested in my well-being, a skilled specialist who had my back. It made me feel okay, worthy, and safe.

It was suggested to me by my treating specialist to write a letter to my five-year-old self, to tell her she is safe now, if I were able. I was able, and I did.

Hello, beautiful girl, you can smile now, you have arrived. When you can, take a deep breath, hold it, and exhale.

Let's surrender together and allow healing to begin.

I want you to know wholeheartedly that I have been paying attention and that I see you.

I and I alone am the witness to your life. I hear your thoughts, I feel your pain, I get you.

Remember when you'd smile. It wasn't often, yet you did. Oh, and do you still love the gorgeous orange nasturtiums in our yard? Suckling the honey from them was so sweet, wasn't it?

Immerse yourself in stuff that feels warm and soft. The stuff that gives you butterflies in the tummy; take notice of those things.

Those butterflies you see and feel, please take notice, observe them, see them, love them. They can be the difference between not feeling anything and feeling joyful and peaceful, to feeling everything.

They are your teachers. Just you wait and see. You will work it out. Warmth will come over you, and tears will rise. Love this feeling. Don't be afraid.

Tears will remind you that you can feel. And these tears will feel warm on your face. Can you feel them? They are there for a purpose. Let me explain a little more.

Rain before rainbows, hard work before results, and pain before relief.

Hurt people, hurt people. Pain hurts, bringing tears. Vulnerability can set in. Somehow, for some reason, thank goodness I've paid much attention, a lot of attention to a process.

And what I now know is that our tears bring relief to our pain. Magic happens when I realise that the painful issue that brought me to tears remains, yet I no longer drown in it. Love your tears, please.

You will see many changes come and go. And they will.

This place is currently a temporary address, a temporary house, temporary advisers, and no more brutal punishments.

I can tell you that the fear in your life in your small hands, those shaky little hands, and the swirling in your tummy and mind will all disappear.

I give you my promise: eventually, when you are older, you will be able to breathe a little easier. Have faith in me, have trust in me, hear my words of wisdom.

You can be free.

I understand the depths of your knowing. You are a very special child to me, immersed in turmoil, awake to it all.

There, lives within you a Resilience, the ability to walk through fire after exploding fire, armed with what it takes to tackle what's next.

There, that resilience lives within you. Don't try to make sense of it all, darling girl. It's impossible to try to make sense of something that doesn't make sense.

You will, in your own time, fall then rise and then do it all again. It is within you to survive the brutal fabricators, the frauds, the fakers, and the false storytellers.

Make sure you listen to your instincts, as those little butterflies are your guides.

Embrace all your idiosyncrasies; Love them; Be brave enough to live them proudly.

Your sense of humour was and remains the key to your survival, to living in your body with some comfort.

Your awareness and insight for someone so young are both worthy and cruel. Your sense of humour and your understanding of it are your gold in the sand.

It truly is medicine for your soul.

And you will find your tribe: your doctors, your dentists, your schoolmates, your friends, and even workmates. Please don't rush into any of it, especially the life partner's thinking. You will know in your body when something or someone is right for you. And when it isn't. You will know it.

Rise from mistakes, they're opportunities to learn and do something different the next time.

Be surprised at your abilities, just like you would show surprise and elation at a friend's abilities; what you do matters.

I care. I will continue to witness your life. I am your lifeline should you ever need to reach out.

Know I adore you. I love you always.

My recovery via the right and proper medication, trust, and safety were the keys to my path of feeling my way to a better me. I was on a journey to discover the missing parts of myself.

What a fantastic team the registrar and doctor were. The therapy took on many versions of healing. I stared closed-minded, argued my points of view solemnly yet vigorously, screwed up my face a lot when I could not find words to suit my feelings, cried, leaned forward and back, and many times dropped my head looking down a lot, shook my head, and sighed at least twenty times each session. I was difficult at times, no question.

Yet I liked my support team, I felt their investment. I was invested too. Perhaps my investment didn't appear, but I realised I needed help. I asked for help, and here I was, bang in the middle of what help looked like. I had not been here before, so I didn't know what it looked like, and I was finding out really quickly.

Accepting the situation I was finally in, and receiving the help I had asked for, was exceptionally hard...bloody hard. All of it. I did not like everything I was hearing from the specialist. All true, yet all hard to stomach. I was suffering from complex post-traumatic stress syndrome and major depressive disorder, the effects of which had my walls built so high that I locked people and feelings out of my world. I knew this, but hearing it from medical professionals is a different story. Now it all had become real. I needed to accept the facts. I had suffered in silence for too long, and those long years of traumatic anguish had made my body sick, and now depression had set in. I needed more help.

My ongoing trauma made my body and mind sick. Very sick.

Therapy continued to tire me. It was what I needed, yet I found it unbearable at times. Hearing proven scientific facts of the effects of extensive physical illness I had due to emotional pain felt like I had made myself sick. I'd let myself down.

I learned to stop blaming myself. I knew I did not cause my childhood pain and needed stoicism, to take a hard line with myself to break free from where I unknowingly had placed the blame for my lack of "living" my life in a way I so wanted and deserved.

I breathed into the little girls inside, the five-year-old and thirteen-year-old me. My psychiatrist wanted to know all about the little peacemaker, beaten, flogged, betrayed, and left picking up her clothes from the front lawn to become a foster kid of sorts. The little girls inside, whom I grieve for every day.

The bravest little girls I've ever met.

I was now their protector; no one would hurt them again. They are mine; they were my reason. I was going to re-raise them both and me, together.

All the things in therapy from then on, all that was essential to my and their well-being and recovery, were not that hard after all. The deep stuff, the stuff I remained clueless about, the stuff that took me way back. It was painful, nauseating, and draining, and beautiful, exhilarating, and soulful, and I did it and still do it for them both and for me.

I slept well one night soon into therapy. The next day, my mind began to loop through memories once again.

The crisp white shirt...the crisp white collar.

The long narrow staircase...the act...one man leaving the room...She did not know what he had done to me, nor what the other man had done. She did not know about that either. Nor the others. I told nobody.

The...urgency in the kiss...the urgency...

The blue suit coat, and the voice, "Hello!"...the kiss on my head...

Unbelievable, the most incredible coincidences? I think not!

Kelvin and Greg! How? What?

Why me?

The man, the teacher I knew on the footpath...really?

The Tradie and the toasty. How did I end up alone in the house when he arrived! Was this a coincidence, again? Alone, when a man arrives wanting sex. He knows, but I do not know. My mother does not know what he wanted apart from fixing the washing machine. She would either help me or not believe me about the men, and I could not risk telling her ever.

Mr Bilson…who took a woman away, leaving her own daughter alone every night, alone in their home…

Therapy and talking, talking, talking!

I was so tired from all the therapy, talking, talking, talking. I loved it, and I did not.

It was so tiring, exhausting!

There was no single ah-ha moment; instead, it was a gradual process, and on one day and the next, the jigsaw of my life became infused with the belief that I am okay just as I am. It was not my fault, my childhood. I lived it, survived it, stood up to it all! I am a survivor!

That belief, that feeling of tingling love inside me, is the very thing I consider that unlocked my mind, brought down my walls. The trust and faith my psychiatrist placed in me, combined with my own confidence and belief in myself, finally unlocked the vault that held the jigsaw puzzle pieces. I visualised the pieces of the puzzle, which began floating back and forth until they finally fit into place.

It was mid-afternoon, the week after I entered the Health Clinic. I sat up and leaned forward on my beautiful, soft, comfortable bed. I took a pillow from behind me and leaned onto it. I think I went into shock. I put my head on my pillow.

The lifelong, mind-altering, excruciatingly painful jigsaw was complete.

Finally, with the pieces aligned, the puzzle of my life felt complete, not perfect, not untouched, but truly mine. Every memory, every scar, every injustice had its place, its purpose, and its part in the design. I could finally see the tapestry of survival, resilience, and love that had carried me, often unseen, for decades.

And with that understanding came a quiet, almost imperceptible freedom, the knowing that I had endured, that I had survived, and that whatever the future held, it was mine to shape.

It was in the stillness after the storm of remembrance that I began to sense the following pieces, which were not yet fully revealed but waiting patiently for me to notice them. The journey was far from over, but the path forward suddenly became clearer, lit by the hard-won light of truth and self-knowledge.

The jigsaw finally came together. Every piece that had drifted in and out of my mind for years finally fitted into place, creating the one picture I had spent half my life fearing, resisting, and searching for.

And with that picture came a truth so staggering and violently confronting that my body reacted before my mind could fully keep up. I felt the shock before I understood. I felt the nausea before I found words. I felt the collapse before clarity settled in.

For the first time, I finally saw not just what had happened to me, but who stood behind it.

That realisation didn't come gently. It tore through me.

Unsent Letter

Dear Little One

You know you were never able to put a puzzle together

Too many pieces

Too many of everything, thoughts, end bits, cardboard boxes

So, you stopped trying

Your brain simply doesn't work that way!

Except, today you did a puzzle!

-50-
I Knew The Who

I never wanted to place the blame there. Ever. There were people in my life who cared for me and those who didn't, and still, I could not understand why.

I was in the hospital, thank God, when the realisation hit me like a truck. Thank goodness I had people around me who cared for me.

I sobbed in disbelief, staring and yelling into my pillow, before feeling numb. My nurse came into my room.

I sobbed as I spoke, now fully supported by the nurse and my treating psychiatrist. I managed a few words with both of them, then lay down, exhausted and in shock.

I woke the next morning, still feeling groggy. I was encouraged to write down what I couldn't say. I tried to write about it, I cried about it, and at times, I wanted to be alone with it.

The words I couldn't speak settled inside me like wet cement, heavy, cold, and moulding themselves around everything I thought I knew. The truth was no longer just at the edges of my mind; it had settled, solid and unmoving. And now I had to live with it.

Those first hours after the realisation were a blur of tissues, shock, and the quiet company of people who refused to let me fall through the cracks. My nurse stayed with me longer than she needed to. My psychiatrist spoke softly, guiding me back to my breath each time I drifted too far into panic.

But when the room finally fell silent, and I was left alone with the truth, I realised something else: this was not an ending. This was the beginning of understanding.

The next morning, still foggy, I picked up the pen they'd left on my bedside table. Writing felt like dragging words through mud. Every sentence tasted like salt. But the page didn't judge me. It didn't ask questions. It didn't interrupt. It simply held what I could no longer keep inside me.

And as I wrote slowly, painfully, and honestly, I felt the next part of the story rising inside me.

What followed was not gentle.

It wasn't easy. But it was essential.

As I sat there with the last pieces of the jigsaw finally in place, the picture wasn't just clear; it was blinding. All the shadows I'd lived with, and all the nights I'd spent wondering who and why, suddenly weren't shadows anymore. They were faces, familiar faces. Faces I had trusted, feared, avoided, loved, and sometimes hated all at once.

And as each name came to mind, that old phrase I'd heard a thousand times echoed back to me, now useless, heavy, and hollow.

Unsent Letter

Dear Lee

Nailing puzzles now, kid!!

-51-
You Never Know

I remember my mother's friend, Anna, regularly responding to questions with, "You never know." Well, I do know now.

That phrase no longer holds any meaning for me. The jigsaw finally gave me the answer to my years of wondering, to the question I was too afraid to name.

I kept replaying the faces, the rooms. Even the smell of stale cigarettes in our lounge room clung to my hair long after everyone had gone home. And with each piece of memory, another possibility surfaced.

It could have been Anna. She was drinking with my mother, pretending not to notice when I left the room as their laughter turned sharp and brittle. She knew what was happening. Maybe she thought she was helping. Perhaps she believed she was saving me from something. Or maybe she wasn't helping at all.

It could have been Vivienne Carlisle, my mother's boss. Perhaps she was tired of my mother bringing me into the hotel so often, plonking me down while she finished her paperwork. Maybe she wanted to teach my mother a lesson, to remind her who was in charge. I don't think she thought of me much anyway. But no, it wasn't her.

It could have been the stalker, the one who sent the letter I never mentioned or answered. Maybe he wanted revenge. Perhaps he believed he had a right to a part of me.

It might have been my father. He was unpredictable and cruel in ways that never made sense. Calling me names, then pretending he never said them. If it were him, it would have been the performance of his life; he loved theatrics. Yet something in me still whispers: he wouldn't have stooped that low.

I couldn't have expected my mother to treat me this way, nor could I have suspected she would. I rescued her from my father. I tended to her after traumatic floggings and even smaller beatings. No, she wouldn't.

It might have been Greg, that annoying boy from school, who kept finding ways to contact me years later. The one I never responded to. Maybe rejection turned to resentment. Perhaps he finally wanted me to listen. He couldn't have orchestrated all of it; he was high most of the time, he said. Still, it could have been him.

Was it Mr. Bloody Bilson? He never thought I was a good enough daughter. Was he punishing me? I doubt it. But maybe it was the softly spoken man who pretended to be a good father and friend.

Anna again. It could have been Anna. She was inebriated most of the time, and hell only knows who she spoke to for hours and hours on the phone, or what she said. Maybe she had the wrong girl and sent the men by mistake; far-fetched, but she was capable of anything with a belly full.

Was it Jon? I did hit him. Fight him. Was he still angry?

Tim was the gross friend of Bertie the Bee. I can't say it was him, but I did think he was among the mix of men I fought and told on, causing the horrid family feud.

It could have even been Penny the Prickle, who couldn't stand the sight of me. Maybe she wanted to leave a mark that lasted longer than her words ever could. However, no, she was too selfish to put in that sort of effort for me.

Would Hughes punish me for not giving him that last goodnight kiss he leaned in for? He wouldn't put me in such a position. He was still teaching, after all. Would he? Were the men his mates? Surely not.

Bertie and Sam were absolutely crazy enough to do anything at all, to me, with their long history of bad ideas and twisted philosophies. My mother and father would have choked them if they'd arranged for men to confront me.

I kept turning the names over, trying them on like costumes, seeing which one fit best. But only one person knew all my weaknesses. Only one person knew how to make me doubt myself, yet still pull me back for comfort.

In the monumental investigation, I lost interest. It was exhausting and emotional, with the findings and evidence hard to hear.

It could not be Anna.

It wasn't Vivienne.

Not Hughes, nor Jon.

Not Mr bloody Bilson.

Not my father, nor Greg.

And not Penny the Prickle.

When I ran out of names, I was left with the one person I never thought to question.

-52-
My Soul Seller

For decades, I had turned over every possibility in my mind. Anna. Vivienne. Greg. Mr Bilson. My father. Penny the Prickle. I had tried them on like masks, testing each face, each gesture, each whisper in memory, hoping somehow that one of them would bear the weight of the truth. None of them did. None of them fit.

And then the memory hit me, sharp and unrelenting, like a wave breaking over rocks. It wasn't distant. It wasn't someone I could push away. The betrayal wasn't a shadow lurking somewhere else. It was closer. So close that I had never imagined it could be possible.

It was my mother.

My own mother. The woman I had loved, the woman I had needed, the woman I had trusted above all. The person who had carried me, fed me, held me when I was small, had been the one to sell my peace, barter my body, and exchange my soul as if I were nothing more than a commodity.

The disbelief hit first. My mind scrambled. How could it be her? The one I saved, the one I loved and tried to love, the one I learned from.

But then the pieces began to line up in a sickening clarity:
the small disappearances, the late-night excuses, the times
I had been left alone, vulnerable, and confused. Every
doubt, every moment of fear, every lingering question of
'Why me?' The answer had been there all along.

I saw her face in every memory, every moment that had
seemed ordinary. The smiles she gave, the irregular, gentle
touches, the words of hope; suddenly, they were hollow,
layered with a darkness I could barely bear to name.
I had never imagined such duplicity could come from
someone I had called "Mum".

And yet, there it was. The truth was undeniable. The
person who had orchestrated my torment, who had
traded my innocence for her gain, was the person I had
loved most.

All the questions I had asked myself for decades now
collided in a torrent of pain. Who found ways to turn
me into something useful? Who needed better financial
security? Who had the power to exchange me like articles
of trade?

She did.

It was my mother.

The revelation left me trembling, exhausted, and
shattered. For the first time, I understood the full
magnitude of the betrayal, the depth of the wound, the
scale of the loss. The answer I had been searching for my
whole life had been right in front of me, hidden in plain
sight. And now, there was no turning back. I had to face
the reality, as unbearable as it was, and confront the truth
of who had sold my soul.

Unsent Letter

Dear Me

'I just died...

and someone else has to learn how to live.'

www.ingramcontent.com/pod-product-compliance
Lightning Source LLC
Chambersburg PA
CBHW032047050726
47590CB00001B/164